Employ Your
GIFT

The Secret to
Living Your Purpose

TJ GILROY

Published by: TMG Associates Press

First Printing: 2019

ISBN: 978-1-7333377-2-4 (paperback)
ISBN: 978-1-7333377-3-1 (ebook)

www.JoePurpose.com

Joe Purpose is a registered trademark of TMG Associates, LLC

Ordering Information:

Special discounts are available on quantity purchases by corporations, associations, educators, and others. For details, contact the publisher at www.JoePurpose.com.

Printed in the United States of America

Contents

Introduction

I grew up with good parents who loved me. I received a good education and went to a good college. I had the career I wanted and married the woman of my dreams. I lived in a good house and drove good cars. Life was good.

But something was missing. After being turned on to books about success principles, I discovered I had no purpose. The more I looked for my purpose the more frustrated I became. I read everything I could get my hands on that related to purpose, only to receive a good understanding of what purpose was without any idea of how to find mine.

I listened to pastors and Bible teachers who often spoke about purpose, and one of them even wrote an all-time bestselling book about the subject. It was good information, but again, no one could tell me how to find my purpose. It seemed as if God miraculously revealed His purpose to some special people, but not to everyone. That didn't sit right with me and was not consistent with the God I knew. I was frustrated because I didn't just want to know about purpose, I wanted to know mine!

Somewhat by accident, I discovered that I was searching for the right thing but in the wrong direction. Finding your purpose is not the beginning; it is the middle of one's quest. Before you can discover your purpose, you need to know what your heart desires. The secret to the desire of your heart is finding your Special GIFT.

Everyone has a Special GIFT, a desire of your heart, and a purpose. They are not miraculously revealed to some and not others; everyone is born with them. The desire of your heart is to use your Special GIFT. Your purpose is to employ it.

1

I found this answer buried in a success book, but Saint Peter said it best:

"As each of you has received a special gift, employ it in serving one another as good stewards of the manifold grace of God."
1 Peter 4:10

This is not just some "religious speak" for churchgoers. It is sage wisdom that has been hidden in plain sight for two thousand years.

As you read on you will discover that this is not a "how-to" book. It is an introduction to the concept that each person has a Special GIFT. I hope that learning this gets you excited, hopeful, and curious; excited that there is something special inside of you, hopeful that it will provide answers to questions you have always had, and curious to discover your specific Special GIFT. Discovering your specific Special GIFT requires some effort, and my desire is for this book to act as a catalyst to spur you to make that effort.

Chapter 1
What I'm Going to Tell You

First, a Story

I live in central North Carolina near the village of Pinehurst. Our area is known for two things: golf and our proximity to Fort Bragg. Pinehurst has several well-known golf courses, and people from all over North America visit here to play a round or two. From my living room window, I can look on to two of those courses and critique the swings of the golfers' tee shots—as if I have any room for criticism. What is especially fun is trying to pick out our visitors from Canada. They are the ones playing golf in shorts in December and January.

Pinehurst is also known as a community near Fort Bragg. If you aren't familiar, Fort Bragg is the home of the Army's 82nd Airborne Division and Army Special Forces. So, we have paratroopers and special operations Green Berets in this part of North Carolina. Many of them fit right in with the local southern population because they enjoy the outdoors so much. Pickup trucks, fishing poles, hunting rifles, and golf clubs are a normal part of the landscape around here.

I bring up what our area of central North Carolina is like to tell you the story of three high school friends who were fishing on a nearby lake. Joe Purpose, who went by Joey (the ringleader); Robert Right, who went by Bobby (the smart one); and Fred Feckless, known as Freddie (the funny one) were out in their bass boat one summer day enjoying life while they fished.

The fish weren't biting, and things got a little boring, so Joey started a conversation to liven things up a bit. "Bobby, what do you think the best invention of all time is?" asked Joey.

"Well, Joey," said Bobby, as he reached for the phone in his back pocket, "I'd have to say it's the smartphone. It has really increased my productivity, and it has more computing power than what the engineers used to send men to the moon. What about you, Joey?"

"I'd have to say it was the Cadillac," said Joey. After a few puzzled looks from his friends, he continued. "That Cadillac leather, and the way they make their back seats, is perfect for making out with your best girl!"

After everyone stopped laughing, Joey looked at Freddie. Besides being the funny one of the three, Freddie would always surprise them. "Freddie, what do you think the best invention of all time is?" asked Joey.

Freddie thought for a few seconds and then said, "The Thermos."

Bobby said, "All right, I'll bite. Why the Thermos?"

Freddie answered, "Well, it keeps cold things cold and hot things hot, right?" Both Joey and Bobby nodded, not knowing where this was going. Freddie continued, "So, **how do it know**?" Freddie was serious, but the other two busted out laughing.

Keeping the conversation going, Joey said, "**Just imagine.**"

"Imagine what?" asked Bobby.

"Just imagine if all this water was beer," said Joey with a chuckle.

"Well, that would change a few things, wouldn't it?" said Bobby, to which Freddie chimed in saying, "Yup, we'd have to start peeing in the boat."

You might be wondering what my story of these three guys on a fishing boat has to do with anything. It is to make two points:

- First, **just imagine**! No, not that your local lake was made of beer, but just imagine that you really had a Special GIFT. How might that change things for you.?

- And second, **how do it (you) know**? Unless someone tells you that you have a Special GIFT, how would you know? How would you know that your GIFT was special and how would you find it?

What I'm Going to Tell You

Attending Marine Officer Candidates School (OCS) in Quantico, Virginia, was a formative time in my early adulthood. It was a "boot camp" for future Marine officers. One of the things I remember from OCS was a drill instructor getting up on stage to address over 200 officer candidates on how to lead Marines. To be honest, I don't remember any of his lesson, but I do remember how he said he was going to teach us. He said:

"First, I'm going to tell you what I'm going to tell you."

"Next, I'm going to tell you."

"Then, I'm going to tell you what I told you."

Stay calm, this is not a "boot camp." I only bring up this memory to let you know that this chapter is the part where I tell you what I'm going to tell you. I have found that giving you a glimpse of what to expect may be helpful. It may keep you engaged while I set the tone with some background information in the early chapters—information you will need for it all to make sense. Telling you what to expect will also give you a sense that this is going somewhere, and that it is worth persevering until the end.

You Have a Special GIFT

Everyone has a Special GIFT; you are born with it. Your GIFT is *Special* because you are the only person with it. Your Special GIFT is unique to you. Your Special *GIFT* is capitalized to differentiate it from other gifts. Your Special GIFT is the one talent you possess that stands out above all your other talents, and that can be developed into greatness. It is a natural part of who you are. But...your Special GIFT is more than talent; it is your unique way of thinking. Your Special GIFT must be discovered and developed.

Sadly, most people go through life without ever realizing that they have a GIFT. That's because they don't really know who they are. You will not find your GIFT if you don't know the real you. God made you who you are on purpose and with purpose. Nothing about you is an accident. So, no matter what you may think, or have been told, the real you is awesome.

The biggest reason that you may not know the real you is what I call a Father Fracture. As I will explain later, we all get our identities from our fathers. This can be a problem. In your formative years, your father is supposed to be your source of protection, your source of provision, and your source of trust. He is supposed to teach you how to play, how to take risks, and how to empathize with others. He is supposed to love you unconditionally, providing you with confidence in who you are, and giving you real self-worth. But what if your dad didn't provide you with those things, what if he wasn't there for you, or what if you never knew your father? What if the whole idea of a father makes you feel abandoned, rejected, fearful, or angry? Then from where do you get your confidence?

The fact is that many people have never known unconditional love and approval from a father. They have no idea what they are missing—a real sense of identity, not based on performance, but on who you are. As Freddie said, "**How do it know**?" How can you know unconditional love and acceptance when you have never experienced it? How can you know this vital part of your identity if you don't know it is missing? It is a vital part of being able to discover your GIFT.

It seems that most of us are prone to drifting through life until something pushes us to the realization that there must be a better way. I call that "something" a catalyst. Most people need a catalyst to make the effort to find their GIFT. Whether your catalyst is some tragedy that makes you hit bottom or someone who does something good for you, or you just hear the truth that you actually have a GIFT, we seem to need something to wake us up and try something different. This book might just be your catalyst.

Employing Your GIFT Is Your Purpose

Everyone should want to know their purpose. Finding out why you were born and what you are supposed to do with your life is something we have all thought of at some point in our lives. But to many, the whole idea of purpose is scary. It is a heavy subject, and what if your purpose is not what you want it to be...then what?

That's why I created the Joe Purpose® character. Joe Purpose is the personification of Your Purpose. He is fun, excited, and optimistic about his vision for the future. Joe helps to take a heavy subject and make it lighter, maybe even fun. That's why he is on the cover of this book. Discovering your Special GIFT should be fun and exciting. It is the key step in finding your purpose.

Once you discover your GIFT, then finding your purpose is easy. My simple, yet effective definition is that *employing your GIFT is your purpose*. I could have also said that *using* your GIFT is your purpose, which would also be true, although not as complete.

When you start to use your GIFT, you will quickly discover that your income is directly related to the time you spend using your GIFT. You will find that employing your GIFT will be much more profitable, more fun, and less stressful than doing other things you may be good at, or things you just have to do to make a living. You can become great at your GIFT, but not at those other things, so your greatest value comes from employing your GIFT.

Another interesting part of discovering your GIFT is that you will naturally want to use it. In other words, you will have a natural desire to use your GIFT. One of my favorite questions to ask people is, "What do you do?" They will normally tell me their occupation. Then I'll ask them, "What do you really want to do?" That's when the answers get interesting.

Some will reply, "You mean, whenever I grow up?" That is code for, "I am too embarrassed to tell you I don't know." Most people just come right out and say, "I wish I knew." The point is that most people can't put a finger on what they desire. Consequently, they end up chasing things they only thought they wanted or chasing what everyone else said they should want.

As you continue to read you will discover the biggest reason that people don't know their Special GIFT is that they don't know who they really are. When you know who you really are, what everyone else says or thinks becomes much less important to you. And when you know your GIFT, knowing what you want becomes natural. You will find you have a natural desire to give your GIFT. This is where passion begins to show up.

Passion is the ability to endure hardship in pursuing your desire. It helps you get around, over, or through obstacles that would stifle those without desire and passion. Passion is natural to those that know their GIFT.

Operating in Your GIFT Is What Makes a Difference

It seems that the subject of Purpose can be overwhelming to some, and the idea of having a GIFT can be too "spiritual" to others, but who doesn't want to make a difference? The real question is, "HOW do you make a difference?"

Since making a difference is such a universal desire of people, the concept has almost become a cliché. If you do even a casual search on the internet you will find every kind of organization imaginable claiming to make a difference. Volunteer organizations, businesses, churches, and political organizations all tell you that they can help you to make a difference. Some of these are worthy causes while others are outright wacky. How can you determine which of these, if any, are outlets for you to make a difference? Without knowing your GIFT, you can't.

The way you were born to make a difference is by applying your GIFT to your desire. For some, that means starting your own cause. You may be a visionary leader who others will follow in a cause that will make a difference for multitudes. But for most people, you will want to find the right cause to follow: a vision that needs your GIFT and that you want to become a part of.

For some, applying your GIFT will have a direct impact on others and that is how you will want to make a difference. Maybe you are GIFTed in healing people physically or emotionally and you can directly impact the lives of many people. Maybe you are a GIFTed musician who directly impacts people with your music. For others, applying your GIFT may enable you to create enough income to fund a vision or a cause. You might make an impact on the company or organization that you work for, and your compensation provides more than you need. You might find that creating wealth enables you to have influence and support worthwhile causes, and this is how you can make a real difference.

9

Everyone is supposed to make a difference. It is not enough for us to drift through life, surviving from one paycheck to the next with a little entertainment to distract us from really living. But you already knew that. The journey to really living and making the difference for which you were born starts with waking up and realizing there is more. You have a Special GIFT, employing it is your Purpose, and operating in it is how you were designed to Make a Difference. **Just imagine** the possibilities!

The Shopping Cart Method

As we get started I'd like to set some ground rules. Throughout the following chapters, I will reference some sources to back up my information. Some of these will be statistics from trustworthy sources, some will be from books written by business authors, some will be from books written by religious authors, and some will be from the Bible.

While I am trying to get you to think differently about your GIFT and how to use it, I am not trying to persuade you to belong to a certain political or religious affiliation. I bring this up because many people today are preconditioned to cringe whenever someone quotes from the Bible. To deny the fact that the Bible contains wisdom that has stood for thousands of years is to be intellectually dishonest.

I recommend that in reading this book, or any other valuable information for that matter, you use the "shopping cart method." When you go to the grocery store you probably get a shopping cart (a "buggy" if you live in the South) to make carrying your groceries easier. As you go down the aisles of the store you put what you can use in your basket and leave what you don't want or can't use on the shelves. If the store carries something you don't like you probably don't leave the store in disgust, do you?

I recommend you do the same thing here. Take what you can use now and leave the rest. You can always come back and revisit the areas you don't agree with or don't like, or you can forget about them altogether. It would be a shame to miss something that could make a difference for you because one part disagrees with you.

Not for Everyone

Before I go on, I need to interject a disclaimer.

While I firmly believe that discovering and developing your GIFT is for everybody, this section may not be for you.

If you have received a GIFT, then there must be a GIFT Giver. I fully realize that some of you who may be reading this are offended by the mere mention of God. If that is you please skip this section. It is not my intention, or my GIFT, to persuade you otherwise.

Someone, whether well-intentioned or not, may have offended you by shoving religion in your face, disappointed you somehow, or outright hurt you regarding God. For that, I am truly sorry, but again, I am not trying to get you to change your mind.

On the other hand, many of you reading this claim to believe in God and may even call yourself a Christian. For you, I am not, in any way, trying to persuade you to change your beliefs or alter them in any way. Again, that is not my GIFT. So, whatever denomination you belong to, or if you have no denomination, this section is for you.

We live in a time of revelation. Whether you call it the information age, or the cyber age, or any other term for this age, we have more information available to the average person today than at any time in history. Our access to the truth is unprecedented! Unfortunately, so is our access to lies, half-truths, and manipulation. It is each person's responsibility to discern the real truth.

Regarding your GIFT, the age in which we live has tools available to help us reveal the truth about ourselves that previous generations did not have. I will refer to some of these tools, such as the personality and strengths assessments, throughout this book. The tools are there to help you discover things about yourself that you probably already suspected. They are an excellent confirmation to many and a complete revelation to others. They will prove to be invaluable aids in discovering your GIFT.

Many companies and organizations use the same assessment tools I recommend, but for a different purpose. Rather than using them to help you discover the greatness inside you, they use the tools to determine if you will be a good fit for their organization and the position they want to fill. Rather than trying to help you excel, they use these assessments to weed out people who don't fit their mold. When I speak of organizations, they could be a small business, a large corporation, a nonprofit, a political organization, the government, the military, or even a church.

You would think that an organization would want you to know your GIFT so that it could be applied to their business. Sometimes, in great organizations, this is true. Sadly, there are very few great organizations, which means they usually have no interest in you finding your GIFT. There is a reason for that.

When you discover your GIFT you also discover that you have value. However, from the perspective of many organizations, the revelation that you have value can undermine their ability to control you. Your realization that they need your GIFT more than you need them can be threatening to an organization.

Since the advent of the industrial revolution, most organizations want to control your life. They want you to need them. If they can make you feel you need them then they can control how much money you make, how much tax you pay, your healthcare, how hard you work, which jobs are available, which promotions are available, the hours you work, and your vacation time. In a way, they even control where you live, what you eat, and your personal relationships.

BUT (don't you just love *buts*?), when you know your GIFT and your value, you can regain control over a large portion of your life. You become an independent thinker (as opposed to a dependent thinker; one dependent on some organization) and determine your own course. That is why God gave you your GIFT.

God gave you a GIFT so that you would have a unique way to succeed in life. He does not want you to be controlled by organizations that are only interested in power; power derived from you, for without you they would have no power.

The Missing Piece

A group of people got together to discuss my book, *The Joe Purpose Master Key: 7 Steps to Making a Difference by Finding Your Purpose* at a training event. They belong to an active professional development program that is designed to help their businesses grow. A moderator asked the group various questions about things like Purpose, Desire, and GIFT. The conversation was lively and quite revealing.

Some of the group had taken the recommended personality assessment and thought that their GIFT was synonymous with their personality. Others thought they intuitively knew their GIFT because they were successful in their chosen professions. Still, others had studied the concept of Purpose, but freely admitted they did not know theirs.

It became obvious to me that these people were honestly seeking their purpose, had studied other books and sources about purpose, and understood how important finding one's purpose is in achieving success. It also became apparent that they were confused about how to discover their purpose and what their GIFT had to do with it. When asked specific questions about how *The Joe Purpose Master Key* helped them to find their purpose, most of them were vague.

However, one of them was very specific. She had taken both the Personality assessment and the StrengthsFinder 2.0 assessment as suggested in the book. She commented that "suddenly everything made sense" after she understood that her top strength was her GIFT. Finding her GIFT was the "**missing piece**" to finding her Purpose and making a difference.

After listening to this amazing conversation about critically important topics, I realized I needed to do a better job of explaining the concept of your Special GIFT. I know that discovering my GIFT radically changed my life, and in the words of this wonderful woman, it is the missing piece to discovering your Purpose.

You Are a Three-Part Person

The concept of your GIFT can be confusing. One of the reasons for the confusion is your concept of who you are. Whether you realize or not, there are actually three aspects of your being. You are a spirit that has a soul, which resides in a body.

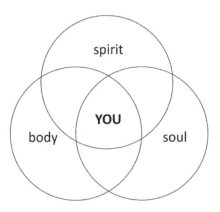

Your body is the physical thing that other people see. They recognize you because of your face, your hair, your eyes...you get the point. It is precisely because your body is how other people recognize you that many people only consider this aspect of who they are. They are more concerned with their weight, their physique, and their age than the more important aspects of who they are.

When I speak of your GIFT, I am not referring to a physical attribute. In other words, I am not referring to how beautiful you are, how fast you can run, or how well you use your hands as a mechanic. While that may be a part of your GIFT, it would be a mistake to call any physical attribute your Special GIFT.

On the other extreme is the part of you that is spirit. Many people have no concept of the fact that they are spirit-beings, and it is not my intention to convince anyone of that fact. I only bring it up because those of you who do recognize your spirit-being may interpret your GIFT as a purely spiritual thing. I believe that supernatural gifts do exist, and they do relate to the way I describe GIFT, but they are not what I refer to when I describe your Special GIFT.

Your soul is distinct from your body and your spirit. Your soul is made up of your mind, your will, and your emotions. Your soul plays a part in who you are as a person with a body and as a spirit. Your soul is completely unique to you and you have complete control over it. Just as your fingerprints, your retinal scan and your DNA (all of which belong to your body) are unique; so is your brain unique to you...no one has a brain just like yours. Since your thinking occurs in your brain, that means your way of thinking is completely unique.

My point is that when I refer to your Special GIFT I am referring to a part of your soul. Your Special GIFT is your unique way of thinking and not to be confused with a supernatural gift or being gifted physically.

"The mass of men lead lives of quiet desperation. What is called desperation is confirmed resignation."
Henry David Thoreau

Chapter 2
It Is What It Is ... or Is It?

Several things come to mind whenever I hear someone say "it is what it is." The 1956 movie *The Man Who Knew Too Much* featured a song by Doris Day called "*Que Será, Será*." The lyrics of the song's chorus are, "Whatever will be will be/ The future's not ours to see." That was my parents' generation's way of saying "it is what it is."

The term "whatever" seems to be a take-off from that theme. Not only does it connote the thought of whatever will be will be, but it also has an underlying tone of indifference. In college polls of 2009 and 2010, *whatever* was voted "the most annoying word in conversation." I completely agree.

The 1988 Bobby McFerrin song "Don't Worry, Be Happy" sort of has the same meaning. However, this song has an upbeat, happy message that always brings a smile to my face whenever I hear it. If you know the song, I'll bet you are smiling right now.

It Is What It Is

I'm not sure of the origins of "it is what it is," but it has been around for a while. It seems to mean the situation stinks but it is out of my control. As one person stated, "It is a super-cool way of expressing apathy wrapped in feigned casualness."

I think Henry David Thoreau expressed the *Que Será, Será/whatever/ it is what it is* sentiment best when he wrote, "The mass of men lead lives of quiet desperation. What is called resignation is confirmed desperation."

This quote perfectly captures the feelings of most people. They feel trapped and desperate. Desperation means having anxiety because of a loss of hope. If you have been taught by your parents, the education system, the government, or even your church that life is meant to be a struggle, where only the toughest or most privileged make it to the top, then what hope do you have? It is what it is, right?

What Is "It"?

"It" is life, and this popular saying infers that you have no control over yours. It means that you are resigned to a life of competition and struggle to get the things you want. It means that you often feel powerless or helpless to fight the larger forces in the world. It means you need to have strong willpower and self-discipline to stay the course. It means you need the right education and skills, and to constantly update them to remain relevant in a fast-changing world.

If you aren't careful this could lead you to believe that without the right skills or the right amount of intellect you are doomed to a life of eternal struggle. It could show up as constantly feeling pressured to update your skills or being required to take continuing education classes to keep up with change that seems to happen at a faster and faster rate. Maybe your struggle to keep up means getting an MBA or a doctorate just so you can keep your job or hope for advancement.

If you have made mistakes along the way you might believe you deserve a cursed life of desperation. I once worked for a business owner who thought he was physically cursed with arthritis and other ailments because of things he had done in his youth. Although he put on a great face at the office, his beliefs hampered his business growth because he felt he had to atone for his past to be successful.

If you are one of the blessed ones, "it" could be really good. You could be blessed with tons of talent, good looks, and intelligence. You were born to the right family, at the right place, at the right time. For you, life is a cakewalk. Since you feel you had no control over your blessings, you might feel sorry for all those less fortunate than you, or you might feel the system is rigged for people as smart and as highly favored as you.

But, if you aren't blessed, then you...

1. accept your fate and resign yourself to that life of quiet desperation,

2. rely on luck—like winning the lottery, which was created just for people who think this way,

3. or hope for a revolution to take away all the stuff the "blessed ones" have.

Whether you think "it" is good or "it" is bad, you have no control. It is what it is!

...Or Is It?

What if you do have control over your life? What if there is a system that you can use to your advantage instead of drifting through life at the whim of other forces? What if "whatever will be" is up to you. What if you already possessed something that enables your success in life?

The answer lies in not trying to fit into a premade mold of what someone else deems as a success. You were born with the ability to control most of your circumstances and determine your success. That is because you were born with what I call a Special GIFT. What you perceive in others as "luck" or being born into a "blessed" life is actually the fact that they learned their Special GIFT and how to apply it.

Using your Special GIFT always enhances your life.

Using your Special GIFT always enhances your life. That is because your Special GIFT is the precursor to your Purpose. It is the source of your passion and it gives you the boldness and confidence you need to enjoy an abundant life. Applying your GIFT means continually developing it, and new revelations come as a result. The effort you put into developing your GIFT is not something you have to do; it is something you want to do. It becomes a labor of love.

Your Special Gift is the one talent you possess that can be developed to greatness. Talent implies a natural ability that comes easily to you. That talent is an expression of your unique way of thinking.

You might think you don't have any talent that can be developed to greatness. I can relate. In high school I was a good student, graduating thirteenth in a class of 625. When I began my studies at the University of Virginia I quickly discovered I wasn't a great student and barely graduated with a B average.

I had a dream of one day becoming a Major League baseball player. I was a good player, making the varsity teams in high school and college. I found out I wasn't a great pitcher when I went to a Major League tryout and didn't last through the first half-hour.

After college, I was commissioned a Marine officer and went to flight school. I was a good officer and a good pilot, good enough to rise above many of my contemporaries, but not really great. I liked my profession, was better than most, but I hadn't discovered my GIFT yet. Everything I did required enormous effort and any success I had up until this point was from being more conscientious and working harder than others.

20

I had, however, become the "go-to" guy for certain things. Whenever there was a difficult-to-solve problem in our unit I was the guy the commanding officer would turn to. Digging deeply into issues and finding solutions came naturally to me. It was a clue about my Special GIFT. If I would have been one of those who said "it is what it is," then I would have thought being good was good enough. But good enough often keeps one from finding their Special Gift.

You are probably the go-to person for something as well. You might not think whatever you are the go-to person for is significant, but people come to you for a reason. When people continually seek you out for help with the same kind of thing, it is an indication of your GIFT. It is because you think about that issue in a special way.

Greatness lies in the unique way you think and your ability to communicate that way of thinking to maximum benefit. It is a natural ability that flows almost without effort. That's because you have a Special GIFT to think that way.

Great engineers think about building things, which is why they became engineers. People who think in terms of data, code, processes, and protocols become great information technology professionals. Great salesmen are masters of psychology and how to influence decisions. That is why they gravitate to sales. Great athletes think about the performance of their body, how to be more effective in their training, and any strategic edge they can gain over their competition. They don't just run faster, jump higher, or are stronger than others. Those things can make someone good, but great athletes think differently.

Albert Einstein was one of the world's greatest scientists. He was a brilliant mathematician and physicist who had a very special way of thinking. He said, "I never came upon any of my discoveries through the process of rational thinking." Most of his brilliant ideas came from what he called "combinatory play." He would often take long walks or play his violin to relax and thoughts would come to him. Then he would daydream about the thoughts, visualizing them until they could be verbalized or put into an equation.

What if Einstein had listened to critics who said he was unconventional? What if he had tried to fit in with the other "rational thinking" mathematicians and physicists? He might have still been brilliant, but would we know him as the greatest theoretical physicist, the one who created E=MC^2 and discovered the theory of relativity? Probably not.

Many people try to struggle through life hoping to make it to sixty-five so they can retire. To them, the idea of having a GIFT probably means it is something you finally get to retire from. WRONG! Your GIFT doesn't dissipate with age.

Consider Ludwig van Beethoven, one of the world's greatest composers. By the time he was thirty, Beethoven realized he was losing his hearing, and twenty years later he was almost completely deaf. If Beethoven had thought "it is what it is," he would have accepted his lot in life and just quit. However, after he became deaf he went on to write some of his most famous music, including the Ninth Symphony with its choral finale. No one retires from their GIFT.

You may not be an Einstein or a Beethoven; in fact, I know you won't. Just as there was only one of them there is only one of you. Your greatness lies in becoming all that your special way of thinking can become. When you become the go-to person you were meant to be, then you will also greatly influence others.

So, the next time you hear someone repeating the mantra "it is what it is," just realize that you have a choice. The choice between a life of struggle and quiet desperation, or a life of passion and purpose by employing your GIFT. You can live by your emotions and feelings or you can discover the unique way you were created to think. Don't resign yourself to accepting "it." You have more control over your circumstances than you might realize.

As you read on you will find out that your Special GIFT can make a way for you, but first you need to understand that no one just drifts through life—you operate within a system.

Chapter 3
Two Systems

When I met my wife, Mary, the way I operated was to take things as they came. After hanging around her for a while I could tell that's not how she operated. Mary always found out what the system was, and then manipulated her way through it, and sometimes around it. I was oblivious to the fact that there was a system. I am really glad she came along to wake me up.

Most of us don't give much thought to how things work in our world; we just live in it. I don't know how a television works, or how I hear radio waves; I just use them. I didn't plan my early Marine Corps career (pre-Mary); I just went with the flow. The challenge with not paying attention to how things really work is that you can assume just because "that's the way it is" that there is no other way...maybe a better way. If you are oblivious to the fact that there is a way that things work (a system), then you may be susceptible to becoming a pawn in someone else's chess game.

While most of us assume there is only one way that the world works, there are actually two different systems at work in your life. One system is based on strife and struggle, and the other is based on your Special GIFT. Understanding both systems allows you to make better choices.

Assumptions: Time and Money

Two of the things that have the greatest influences on our lives are time and money. We spend time to make money, and then spend money to enjoy our time. If those things are so important, it makes sense that we should know the truth as to how they operate. The reality is that most of us take the systems of both time and money for granted and only assume we know something about them.

We all make assumptions...sometimes without even knowing it. For example, what date do you think it is? Our current calendar is called the Gregorian calendar, but that was only instituted in 1582. Pope Gregory changed it from the former Julian calendar, which was different by ten days. That means that if you refer to a date before 1582, there can be as many as ten days difference to today's calendar. If you are trying to determine a date based on this lack of information, your assumption would be faulty. We assume all kinds of things, believing them to be true without giving them much thought.

Have you ever stopped to think about how we measure time? A year is the time that it takes the Earth to revolve around the Sun. Months, weeks, days, and hours are all based on the Sun and Moon. Have those times and distances always been the same? No, they haven't. The path that the Earth travels around the Sun changes, which means that a year today may be different from a year in the past.

What happens to time if you travel in space and you are not revolving around the Sun? According to Einstein's theory of relativity, time is not constant. Did you know your GPS wouldn't work if scientists didn't know that fact and were able to measure it?

One last assumption about time. Is time linear? To most western civilizations we think that time operates in a line. It had a starting point and it travels in one direction. That is where we get the word *timeline*. But to many Semitic cultures, time is a circle. They refer to time in eras or epochs. When one era (or circle of time) ends another one starts. This way of thinking about time puts the concept of life and death in a completely different perspective for those cultures.

When it comes to money, we also make assumptions. Most people think the world has always had money of one sort or another, but that is not true. Bartering was the first way of trading one thing for another. If a farmer had more grain than he needed and someone else had more fish than they needed, they would trade (barter) for what the other person had. Money just made bartering easier.

The first coins were used for money in 600 BC. The first paper currency was probably established by the Chinese around 618 AD, and Marco Polo brought the idea back to the western world around 1300 AD. The whole concept of money was that it represented the value of some commodity (usually silver or gold) that was universally accepted to have value. Most people still believe that is how it works, which lends itself to the idea there is only so much money because there is only so much gold or silver. But that's not true either.

Did you know that almost all world currencies are based on the dollar? So, what is the dollar based on? It used to be gold, but that changed in 1971 when President Nixon took the United States off the gold standard. That means that the US dollar is based on nothing. Money is nothing more than an idea, and the US dollar only has value because we have confidence that it does. What happens if people lose confidence in the dollar—like if we just print it whenever we feel like it?

The point is that we spend a huge portion of our time trying to make money. How we go about trying to accomplish that is often based on our assumptions, but are those assumptions valid? Most of the time our assumptions don't seem to make much difference. The theory of relativity and whether your dollars are based on gold or not probably don't have much bearing on your life right now. However, some assumptions are life-altering. Regarding your Special GIFT, your assumptions make a very big difference.

The World

Depending on the economic conditions, what people want most is either more time or more money. When the economy is good it seems that people want more time. If the economy is not so good, what people really want is more money. How we go about gaining more time and more money is often based on assumptions about our world, many of which just aren't true.

When you refer to the *world*, what does that mean? According to the Merriam-Webster dictionary, *world* means: *the earthly state of human existence.*

When we think of the world we are describing the way things work in our daily lives. The way things work is another way of saying a **system**. If we assume our system is how things have always worked, and will always work, that would be a big mistake.

My eighty-nine-year-old mother was born into a world where almost no one had an automobile, air travel didn't exist, very few people had telephones, and the first computer hadn't been invented. How different was her world then to the world now? Can you imagine how different the world will be eighty-nine years from now? We often assume that the way things are now is how they have always been, and will always be, but that just isn't true.

We have been taught to believe many of our assumptions. From the time you are born to the time you learn to think for yourself, there is a system in place that teaches you how to have your needs met. Whether they are physiological needs (food, water, air), physical needs (bodily safety), emotional needs (friendship and companionship), or financial needs (money to pay the bills for your basic needs), we are taught that what everybody else is doing to meet those needs should work for us.

Psychologists have named all of these needs and grouped them as a means of explaining human behavior. The best-known explanation of human needs is called the Maslow Hierarchy of Needs. Maslow grouped needs into two major categories: Deficiency needs and Growth needs. Those categories were then subdivided to show the progression as needs become filled. Whether you were aware of Maslow and his hierarchy or not, the system he describes is what most of us assume to be true.

According to Maslow, the lower needs must be met first before moving to higher needs. If someone has progressed up the hierarchy, but a lower need now becomes deficient, then that person will act to fill the lower need first before continuing at a higher level.

For example; let's say your current level of need is for achievement and recognition, but a hurricane destroys your home and all your food. Then, according to Maslow, you would divert all your attention to providing food, water, and shelter before going back to fulfilling your need for achievement. This makes perfect sense.

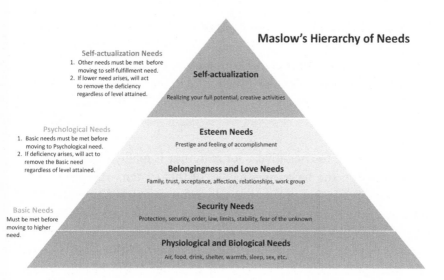

But what happens when one is stuck in the lower levels of the hierarchy? What if life is always a struggle for survival, where putting food on the table and keeping a roof over your head consumes all of your time? What chance would you have to ever feel recognition, search for knowledge, or reach your potential? According to Maslow, it would not be possible.

I call those lower levels of needs Basic needs, which include the needs for food, water, shelter, and security. We all feel the need for security, but how those needs are met makes a very big difference. Your source of security, to a large extent, determines your worldview.

The First System

The First System has a world view that we all move up the needs hierarchy from Basic needs to Psychological needs, to Self-actualization needs. Either we fill those needs ourselves—by our efforts—or someone else provides them for us. In this system relatively few, two percent or fewer, ever find and fulfill their purpose.

Even if you have never heard of Maslow's Hierarchy of Needs, most of us operate in a system that assumes it is correct. The majority of people spend most of their waking moments thinking of nothing but food, drink, the size of their house, staying warm in the winter and cool in the summer, and sex. They are living in the bottom rung of the hierarchy.

Without getting too negative, a lot of money is made from people who are trapped in the basic needs level of this system. Pay attention to the commercials you see on the television or marketing adds on the internet. How many of them have to do with your basic needs? These would be things like food, drink, the house you live in, the car you drive, and yes...sex. Not only do businesses target this level of needs, but so do politicians, as well as some religious organizations. If there is money and power to be had by keeping people at this level, you need to ask yourself why anyone would want to help you rise above that level.

Joe Purpose®

Survival is Nacho Purpose

Just above this is the need for security and protection. This level includes physical security from intruders and protection from invaders. It would also include laws to keep the system functioning in some sense of order, and limits to keep people under control. This level assumes that people only obey laws and stay within limits if they are forced to do so by the system.

Only after these two levels of need are fulfilled would people look to have their needs for love and belongingness fulfilled. This is where the values of family, affection, relationships, trust, and love begin to be valued. This is also where working together as part of a group begins to take place.

Maslow's Hierarchy of Needs

1. Lower need must be met before moving to higher need
2. If deficient in a lower need person will act to remove the deficiency regardless of level attained

The TRAP

Esteem Needs
Achievement, status, reputation, sense of competence, respect of others

"The mass of men lead lives of quiet desperation. What is called resignation is confirmed desperation."
Henry David Thoreau

Belongingness and Love Needs
Family, trust, acceptance, affection, relationships, work group

Security Needs
Protection, security, order, law, limits, stability, fear of the unknown

Physiological and Biological Needs
Air, food, drink, shelter, warmth, sleep, sex, etc.

Whether it is on purpose or by accident, it seems that most of humanity remains trapped in the lower two or three levels of this pyramid. I say it is a trap because the forces that make money at those levels also derive power from it. It is in their best interest to keep as many people as possible in the lower two levels of need, which makes escaping this trap difficult.

Right about now you might be asking yourself what any of this has to do with your Special GIFT or your purpose. Actually, it has everything to do with it, so please hang in there. This is going somewhere, I promise.

We have been taught that there are two ways to succeed (escape the trap). First: You have to work hard, get a great education, and persevere for years. It involves a dream, a huge struggle, and the hope of a prize at the end. If you are blessed to live in a country that allows you to work hard and succeed according to your efforts, then you can achieve as far as your ambition will carry you. You can make enough money to escape the trap of the hierarchy's Basic needs and progress to the Self-actualization needs.

The second way to succeed in this system is to be born into privilege. If your parents or ancestors were successful enough to provide you with an inheritance, then you can skip the struggle and go directly to the higher part of the hierarchy.

You might believe, as most do, that to be wealthy and successful you had a lucky break or you inherited your wealth. But what are the facts? Assuming your definition of being successful is to have achieved millionaire status (a net worth of $1 million or more), then you might be surprised. According to Chris Hogan's book *Everyday Millionaires*, 74% of millennials and 52% of Baby Boomers believe that millionaires inherited their wealth. The facts say otherwise; 80% of millionaires come from families below the middle-class level.

Seventy-six percent of millionaires say that anyone can become a millionaire if they work hard and have some self-discipline. You might be surprised to find out that in 2018 there were 10.8 million millionaires in the United States, an increase of 6% from the previous year. There are about 209 million adults in the United States, which means that about 5% of adults have become successful in this system.

So, what's the point? The adage of "get a good education, get a good job, work hard, and you'll be successful" still works, but there are some caveats. Why are only 5% successful by these terms? How many of the 5% are also successful in their marriages and relationships? How many of them feel fulfilled and have reached their full potential? Are they really successful, or did they just make it to retirement?

The idea that life is a struggle resounds in this First System. The 5% that "make it" will tell you there is no substitute for hard work, diligence, and...struggle. The top 1% of the world's wealthy, many of whom did inherit at least some of their wealth, often feel guilty that they did not have to struggle. That may, in part, explain why some politicians talk about redistributing wealth to those less fortunate than themselves. Of course, those who did struggle and made it to the ranks of the successful rebuke those arguments.

This takes us into a discussion about fairness. Is it fair that some make it out of the bottom levels of the Maslow Hierarchy and others remain trapped? An honest look at history shows that many people have lived under blatantly unfair conditions. Different philosophies have different answers about relieving those who live under unfair conditions, but it is amazing how often the concept of *struggle* comes up.

Karl Marx, the father of communism, wrote about class struggle. Lenin wrote about the working-class struggle. Hitler wrote *Mein Kampf*, translated as *My Struggle*. This is not to say that people don't struggle and that it is often bad, but it is to point out that people in the lower levels of the Hierarchy of Needs can be manipulated by those offering a way out of their struggle. People who are trapped in the lower level of needs, either actually or perceptually, may buy into some pretty radical things to find a way out.

None of the solutions to breaking out of the lower level of needs is based on finding and using your Special GIFT. Either you break out by your hard work and determination or you rely on a government or institution to do it for you. In either case, the statistics of breaking out are not good.

The Second System

The First System is what most of us were taught. It is the system in which we currently operate, and we may not even suspect there is another system. After all, everyone we know is trying to make it this way...aren't they? It is what it is, right?

But what if there was another way? What if the answer wasn't hard work and determination on the one hand or a political solution on the other hand? What if instead of starting at the bottom of the Hierarchy of Needs you could start at the top? Sounds crazy, right?

The Second System starts with the premise that you were born with a Special GIFT.

The Second System starts with the premise that you were born with a Special GIFT. Just as you were born with a unique set of fingerprints, a unique retinal scan, and unique DNA, you were also born with other unique traits. Any parent with two or more children learns early on that their children do not have the same personality. They didn't learn their personality but began displaying it early on without any outside influence. Parents are often amazed at how different their kids can be.

Your Special GIFT is also unique to you, and you were born with it. Because everyone's Special GIFT is different it is not easily developed by a system. Instead, each person has to develop their GIFT independently. There is no "cookie-cutter" solution, which is one of the reasons no one talks about it.

Whereas the First System trains individuals to become part of a group, the Second System is made of unique individuals. The groups of the First System also change over time. A group in the First System during Pope Gregory's time before he changed the calendar probably still believed that the Sun was the center of the universe. Disagreeing with those in control of the system could prove detrimental to your health.

Groups can be manipulated to behave in predefined ways, but that is much more difficult for individuals. Groups can be managed, but individuals have to be led. Because of this fact, the First System has little use for people finding and developing their Special GIFTs.

It seems that very few people are aware of the concept of having a Special GIFT. If we were taught to find and develop our GIFT instead of being educated to find a job to meet our needs for security, our lives would be very different. For the Second System to operate in your life, you first have to realize that it exists, and then you have to seek it.

This is precisely what was meant when Jesus said to "seek first the Kingdom of God and His righteousness, and all these things (basic needs) will be added unto you." If you seek the basic needs first, then you are doing things backwards according to Jesus. His way, established over 2,000 years ago, is to start at the top.

The Second System starts with you finding your GIFT. Once you have been "educated" and helped to develop your GIFT, you can find where your GIFT fits into the system and how it can benefit others. It is your GIFT that will make a way for you and provide for you. Your GIFT will have value in the system because no one will perform your GIFT as well as you and with the same passion.

Where the First System pays money to you based on how much time you spend at a job, the Second System rewards you for the value you bring to the system. Each GIFT is needed and valued, therefore each person is needed and valued. One does not retire from their GIFT and giving your GIFT is what you do. It gives you joy and fulfillment, as well as taking care of your needs.

The First System was created by people with a worldview that struggle was a natural part of the system. Success in this system is based on your effort and you get the credit. The Second System is the Creator's design of how things are supposed to work. He gave you a Special GIFT so that you could enjoy life and give Him the credit.

Even if you are "successful" in the First System, it does not necessarily mean you have fulfilled your purpose. It just means you have risen above survival. Success in the Second System means that you have employed your Special GIFT and have fulfilled your purpose. Now that you know there are two systems, you get to choose in which one you operate.

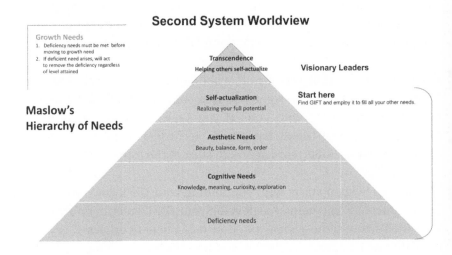

My Assumption About You

The fact that you chose to read this book allows me to make a few assumptions about you. I assume you realize you have a seed of greatness in you, and that you want to find your purpose so that you can make a difference.

Unless you have already found a way to create more than enough money to take care of your basic needs, I assume that you recognize the **need** to make more income. I think if more people were honest with themselves they would admit that more income is really what they are looking for, even more than making a difference.

I also assume that unless you have heard of your Special GIFT before, which is very unlikely, your attempt to create more income probably took the form of:

- Getting a new job

- Getting more education

- Getting a second job

- Working overtime

...or some variation of that theme. I assume that you found those efforts involve struggle and that they don't solve the problem.

The way to create more income and enjoy it is to use your Special GIFT.

Your income is directly related to the time you spend operating in your Special GIFT. This is the key to escaping the trap of the First System and enjoying the life offered by the Second System.

Your Income is directly related to Your GIFT.

Chapter 4
The Missing Piece

A mentor is a trusted counselor or guide according to the dictionary. But the etymology (the word history) of *mentor* has a much more interesting and deeper meaning.

In Greek mythology, *Mentor* was the name of a person in the *Odyssey*, written by Homer. The Odyssey is the story about the travels of King Odysseus after the Trojan War. Before Odysseus departed from Greece to fight in the war against Troy he put Mentor, an old and wise man, in charge of training his son, Telemachus.

The goddess Athena wanted to add her divine counsel to Telemachus, so she appeared to him in the form of Mentor. Disguised as Mentor, the goddess Athena showed Telemachus how to deal with the evil men who wanted to take his father's estate and possessions (his father, Odysseus, being too far away in Troy to defend his property). Athena also appeared in the form of Mentor to Odysseus to give him wise counsel on how to regain his kingdom after he returned from his odyssey.

From this mythology, we see that a mentor is someone who imparts wisdom to and shares knowledge with a less experienced person. I find it interesting that the mythology also implies that Mentor's wisdom had a godly, divine nature to it. Wisdom was imparted through Mentor's form, but it was Athena, the goddess of wisdom, who was providing the advice.

Some people will tell you the best wisdom is experience. I would hope that you do learn from your experiences; however, sometimes you will need the wisdom from a trusted counselor who has experience in something you are going through. As mythology implies, it is a great advantage when your mentor has Godly wisdom.

I have the great fortune to have a mentor in my life. I met my mentor, Jack Daughery, in the Amway business. I was still in the Marine Corps, on my last overseas deployment, when I learned that my wife, Mary, signed us up in Amway. Mary was a naval officer, is super-intelligent, and entrepreneurially minded, so if she thought becoming an Amway distributor was a smart move, then it sounded good to me.

As we both left the military and entered the "real world," I began to realize I knew absolutely nothing about business. I also found that what I thought I knew about leadership changed dramatically when I took off the uniform and people didn't have to do what I told them. I tell you this to let you know that I desperately needed help.

Jack is a self-made multimillionaire who credits his success to learning the principles taught in Napoleon Hill's books, as well as his uncanny ability to read people. I had never heard of success principles or Napoleon Hill before I met Jack, but the more I read the more I grew.

The Quest for Purpose

The foremost principle of success is to have what Hill calls a Definite Major Purpose. I had never heard of Definite Major Purpose before, didn't know anyone who did before meeting Jack, and certainly did not have one myself. So, the quest to find my purpose began.

Now that I was reading about success and had a wealthy mentor, you would think things would start falling into place, right? Not so. The more I tried to apply what Hill wrote the more frustrated I became. I didn't know my desire, couldn't get passionate about anything, and relied completely on my willpower. I was trying to imitate Jack, but we are very different personalities, so that didn't work too well.

I finally summoned the courage to ask him about passion. Jack is very passionate about what he does; it is like he eats, breathes, and lives passion. That is one of the things that draws people to him and scares them at the same time. I thought he was just the right guy to unlock the door for me. Boy, was I wrong!

If you are trying to live with passion but don't possess it yet, you can learn from my mistake. This is one of those rare occasions where the one who has what you want can't help you get it for yourself. When we sat down to counsel about having passion in what I did, Jack looked at me as if I was a Martian (no, that's not a Moron; a Martian...like from Mars). He could not conceive of a person not knowing what they desired and going after it with passion.

I could have walked away from that session to go find someone else to help me, but I didn't, at least not right away. I felt like a real loser. To make matters worse, Jack told me what I needed to do was to just get into a white heat of activity and the passion would follow. That's exactly what Mary wanted to hear. She and Jack have very similar personalities, so this made perfect sense to her.

Once I recovered from my wounds, I asked a couple of other people I thought were passionate how they gained their passion. I received the same dazzled look from them that I got from Jack. They couldn't imagine someone not knowing their desire and going after it.

For whatever reason, I could not resign myself to life without desire and passion. I wanted desperately to put 100% of myself into something that mattered but always walked away disappointed. Rather than giving up, I resolved to figure this out. There had to be a way for anyone to find their desire and live with purpose.

Purpose Isn't the Answer—It Is the Result!

I was trying to find my purpose, but what I needed to do was to discover my desire. In Hill's famous book *Think and Grow Rich*, there is a caption that says, *"Desire is the starting point of all achievement."* That made sense, but the problem was I didn't know my desire, and nowhere does the book say how to find your desire.

> ## "Your major responsibility right now is to find out what you desire in life."
> Napoleon Hill

In another Hill book, *The Master Key to Riches,* he says, *"Your major responsibility right now is to find out what you desire in life, where you are going, and what you will do when you get there. This is one responsibility which no one but you can assume, and it is the responsibility 98 out of every 100 people will never assume. That is the reason why only 2 out of every 100 people can be rated as successful."*

That's when it dawned on me that none of the success principles work until you know what you desire. I asked my mentor, Jack, if that was correct. After admitting he was astonished people didn't know that desire came first, he confirmed that the success principles only work when you have an obsessional desire.

That's when I stopped seeking purpose and began seeking my desire. The first step was to understand what desire was. I had never looked up the word, and you probably haven't either.

Desire
Having a strong persistent expectation for something.

And the word *passion* is related to desire.

Passion

A strong, active, intense, emotional *desire* that enables you to endure hardship, even suffering.

Until I understood what desire and passion were, the only advice I had received was to create so much activity that my desire would reveal itself. When I tried to do that I found it took an enormous amount of self-discipline and was exhausting. I figured that if it took that much self-discipline for me, then most people would not go through the effort required.

In *How to Raise Your Own Salary*, my favorite Hill book, I read this: *"Thought habits can be established only through strict self-discipline..."*

(Oops, it sounds like the answer is back to self-discipline, yuck! But hold on...)

*"It is no trouble at all to form thought-habits if one has **a definite motive, backed by a strong emotional desire** for the attainment of the object or motive."*

I found it comforting to know there was a way to make self-discipline easier and that Hill says DESIRE is the key to self-discipline and habits. BUT, again, **he doesn't tell you how to find it!** Not one book I could find nor any speaker I have heard could tell me how to find my desire. They all start with the assumption you have one. If you will recall, Hill said that only 2% have one, and in mentoring with Jack, we agree it is more like 1%...OR LESS.

The Missing Piece

Jack is an incredibly self-disciplined man. He is disciplined in his thoughts, his health, and with his money. One of the ways he teaches people about making and keeping money is through the books of Robert Kiyosaki. Kiyosaki's *Rich Dad Poor Dad* series of books is a must-read for anyone who wants to make more income and reap the rewards of their income.

It was in a short passage from one of Kiyosaki's books, *Before You Quit Your Job*, that I found my missing piece of the puzzle. He uses conversations with his "Rich Dad" to get his point across to his readers. In one of those conversations Kiyosaki talks about gift:

> **Rich Dad:** *"One of the keys to attracting the invisible magical forces is to be dedicated to giving your gift."*
>
> **Kiyosaki:** *"What?" I responded with a jolt. "Giving my gift? What do you mean by a gift?"*
>
> **Rich Dad:** *"A special God-given talent," Rich Dad replied. "Something you are best at. A talent God gave especially to you."*

On the surface, this passage wasn't that big of a deal—until I linked it with a scripture from the Bible. As I mentioned in the beginning, not recognizing the wisdom of the Bible is being intellectually dishonest.

1 Peter 4:10 says, *"As each one has received a special gift, employ it in serving one another as good stewards of the manifold grace of God."*

There are four points I want to make from this one sentence of Saint Peter:

1. Everyone has received a special gift. This is not a question; it is a statement.

2. What you are supposed to do with your Special GIFT is to employ it in serving others.

3. You are supposed to do it as good stewards. This implies developing and growing your gift.

4. You received your Special GIFT by grace. Grace is not just "religious speak"; it means unmerited, unearned favor. You did nothing to receive your gift, so it's not all about you.

So that was the missing piece. Kiyosaki said it in his book and Peter said in The Book. Your Special GIFT is the missing piece in discovering your Desire and Purpose. Once you know your Special GIFT, you will Desire to use your GIFT and employ it in your Purpose.

My Mission

Once I discovered that the key was this thing I call a Special GIFT, it became my mission. My mission is to change the percentage of people who know their GIFT and are employing it—in other words, change the number of people who live their purpose.

Just imagine! What would happen in an organization if just 5% of the people in that organization were using their GIFTs with passion? The creativity would be amazing. The productivity would be off the charts. They would make more profit and everyone would want to be employed there.

What if just 5% of the country would use their GIFT with passion? What problems could be solved? How much anger would subside? What kind of example could we be to other nations?

Have you ever heard of anyone being depressed who knew their GIFT, lived with Purpose, and was helping others? Me either. What about suicide (which, along with depression, is an epidemic)? Who would want to take their own life if they had a purpose, they were passionate about it, and they were making a difference? No one!

So, my mission is to tell people:

You have a Special **GIFT.** Employing it is your **Purpose**, and Operating in it is the way you **Make a Difference.**

Chapter 5
Foundation

The biggest reason people don't know their Special GIFT is that they don't know who they really are. They might think they do, but often people's perceptions of themselves are based on what others have told them.

Zig Ziglar is credited with creating the concept of BE, DO, HAVE, which goes like this: First, you have to BE. That means being true to yourself and acting from who you are. Who you are will determine what you DO—your occupation or vocation. What you do will be a natural expression of who you are. Then, what you do will determine what you HAVE.

Be – Do – Have

Instead, what we see most often is that people want to HAVE first. They determine what they DO to get what they want to HAVE. The BE part gets left out of the equation entirely. That's why, even if they have a lot of possessions and have the appearance of success, these people are never satisfied. They started in the wrong place and without a foundation of knowing who they are.

Have – Do – ~~Be~~

The key to finding your purpose is to discover your Special GIFT. Your GIFT is the unique way you think, as expressed in the one talent you possess that you can develop to greatness. Everyone has a Special GIFT, but few people ever find it. You see, there is a secret to finding your GIFT. That secret is to know who you really are. Without an accurate answer to that question, the chances of finding your GIFT are remote, which makes finding your purpose, knowing your desire, and making a difference almost impossible. You have to start with the right foundation.

Who Are You, Really?

In my seminars, I start by asking each attendee to take out a sheet of paper and a pen. I ask them to fill in the following statement:

I am _____ (you fill in the blank).

I give group participants fifteen seconds to fill in their answers.

You try it.

Did you finish the statement in fifteen seconds, or did you have to think about it longer? Did your "I am" statement describe your job or title? Did it describe your position in a family? Is that the real you? Did you even try? Caught you!

If you can't state who you are with confidence, and quickly, then there is a very real probability you don't know the answer. If you have to think about who you are, what are you broadcasting to others? Whether you realize it or not, you are sending out signals to those around you that says you don't know who you are. Consequently, they either treat you with indifference, don't know how to treat you, don't recognize your talent, or try to manipulate you. You probably do the same thing to other people who don't know who they are. Wouldn't you agree the "real you" is someone you should know?

Was your response an assumption? Many people assume they are who other people tell them they are. How many times have you heard someone close to you say something like, "You can't do that," or "Who do you think you are?" How much have these comments influenced your opinion of yourself? If that influence took place before you were old enough to reason for yourself, it had a very profound effect.

Psychologists argue about the exact age, but from the time you were born until you were about five or six years old, almost everything you were told by your parents and the authorities in your life went straight into your mind, completely unfiltered. So, do you really know who you are?

The question "Who am I, really?" is not new. In the Sixth Century B.C., Sun Tzu wrote *The Art of War*. In it he said this:

"If you know others and know yourself, you will not be imperiled in a hundred battles; if you do not know others but know yourself, you will win one and lose one; if you do not know others and do not know yourself, you will be imperiled in every single battle."

In 400 B.C., Socrates coined the phrase *"Know Thyself."*

Shakespeare said, *"This above all: to thine own self be true...."*

However, the most important reference in answering this question comes from the Gospel. Jesus said that the entire Gospel was based on two commandments, the second of which is *"Love your neighbor as yourself."* You cannot love your neighbor until you love yourself, and you cannot love what you do not know.

You cannot love what you do not know.

The complexity of our world has made it more challenging today than in the past to know who you really are. In an age where technology doubles every two years, and where there is more change reported in the Sunday edition of a newspaper than during the entire eighteenth century, keeping up can be difficult.

We have more influences on us now than at any time in history. This generation has been marketed to through radio, television, mobile phones, magazines, newspapers, the internet, Facebook, Twitter, and a whole host of new and emerging social media formats. All this marketing, along with the pressures of society, shape how we see ourselves. If you add the demands of worldwide economic upheaval, unemployment, changing moral values, and political unrest, it's no wonder people feel they are living lives of quiet desperation.

You Are Unique

You know better than anyone else just how complex you are. You are unique—a "one-of-a-kind." If you doubt that, let me employ a little of the Socratic Method (asking questions to get you to think) on you.

Does anyone else have your fingerprints?
Does anyone else have your retinal scan?
Does anyone else have your DNA?

The answer is "No" to all three of those questions. You are unique. Your uniqueness extends to other areas that combine to make the real you. Some of these areas include:

Your personality

Your father

Your generation

Your gender

Your thoughts about money

How you give and receive love

Your career

Your ethnicity

Your race

Your socioeconomic status

Your culture

Where you grew up

When you were born

Your environment

Your experiences

Your education

All of these and a whole host of other factors combine to make you the unique person you are. So, on the surface, it may seem an easy question to answer, but on a deeper level, it is very complex.

To help you answer the question, "Who are you, really?" we will explore the top six areas in the list above. Once you have a better understanding of those six, knowing the real you should be within your grasp.

Personality

Have you ever carefully watched small children? Can you pick out how different their personalities are? Most parents who have more than one child will tell you their children are very different from each other, and they noticed the differences soon after birth.

Merriam-Webster's Collegiate Dictionary contains this interesting definition of *personality*:

"The complex of characteristics that distinguishes an individual or a nation or a group; the totality of an individual's behavioral and emotional tendencies; the organization of the individual's distinguishing character traits, attitudes or habits."

So, this definition tells me that how you act, react, organize, and form habits are based on your personality. How you behave is primarily influenced by your personality.

You were born with your personality. In addition to the gift of life, your Creator gave you the gift of your personality. He said, *"Before I formed you in the womb, I knew you."* Each person's personality is perfect for him or her. No one personality type is better than another. You can hide your real personality behind a mask, you can then unmask it, but you cannot change how you were created. Your personality is perfect for you, so why would you want to change it?

Since your personality affects the way you act, how you react to circumstances, how you organize your thoughts, how you form habits, and how you think about things, wouldn't it be a good idea to understand your personality as well as you can?

DISC Personality Assessment

Several institutions have developed excellent methods for testing and categorizing personalities. The one I recommend is the DISC profile assessment. It is based on your answers to a few questions, and it is incredibly accurate! Taking the assessment takes only a few minutes and it will benefit you for the rest of your life. As the DISC people are fond of saying, "Why guess when you can know?" You can learn more about where to find the DISC assessment tool in the Resource Section.

DISC is an acronym that is a combination of the four major personality types. They are the Dominant, Influencing, Supportive, and Cautious personality types.

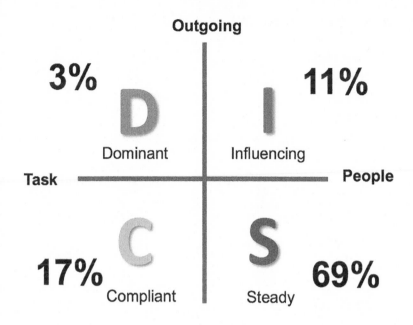

"D" style people are:

    Dominant

    Directing

    Demanding

    Doers

The D personalities are driven people and represent about 3% of the population. They are forceful in demeanor, and likely measure their success in life by wins and losses. They want to be in charge, they exert control, and they want to win. They get things started and keep them moving. They write books about goals, measure achievement by goals, and think everyone else should also. They are the least likely personality style to believe one's personality makes any difference because everyone should be like them. They are the most likely personality style to be natural leaders.

D personalities tend to see themselves as...

> Pioneering
>
> Adventurous
>
> Upbeat
>
> Competitive
>
> Fearless leaders

People who are not D personalities tend to see D personalities as...

> Domineering
>
> Abrasive
>
> Rough
>
> Firm
>
> Risk takers

"I" types of personalities are:

> Influencing
>
> Inspiring
>
> Impulsive

About 11% of the population has I as their dominant personality trait. I type personalities love to be around people, and they think everyone should like them. They like to be the center of attention and are usually very charming and fun to be around. I personalities are infamous for acting or talking first and thinking later. If they have to bend (or completely ignore) the facts to inspire someone they have no qualms about it. If they make a mistake it would not be uncommon to hear them say something like, "It's okay, they'll still like me."

I once had a boss named Charlie (actually, he was the president of the company) who was a very high I personality. Charlie loved going on sales calls and working at trade show booths, and I learned a lot from him. Charlie was one of the most liked people in his industry and everyone knew him. However, on some sales calls I went on with him I wanted to find a hole and climb in because of some of the stuff he would say. If he was asked a question about a product that he didn't know, he would just make up things. He said it so convincingly, and with such great enthusiasm, that people just believed him. I remember calling him on it once, and he looked at me as if to say, "What's the big deal?"

I personalities see themselves as...

> Upbeat
>
> Fun
>
> Enthusiastic
>
> Optimistic
>
> Persuasive
>
> Spontaneous

Other people sometimes see I personalities as...

> Overly confident
>
> Unrealistic
>
> Talkative
>
> Poor listeners
>
> Self-promoting
>
> Exaggerating
>
> Unpredictable

The "S" style of personality:

The S Style is the most common of the four major styles. Approximately 69% of the population exhibits the S style as part of their dominant personality blend. They are people oriented and reserved in demeanor.

Words that describe an S personality are...

> Supportive
>
> Steady
>
> Sensitive
>
> Stubborn

They like to belong to a team, they resist change, and they don't want to rock the boat. They are great employees and crave peace and security. They want to be appreciated and to have a voice. S personalities like to build relationships, and they tend to think with their emotions. If pushed into a corner, the S personality can be very stubborn and be willing to fight, but they prefer peaceful solutions.

S personality types see themselves as...

> Considerate
>
> Good listeners
>
> Calm
>
> Easygoing
>
> Kind
>
> Team players

However, other personalities can see them as...

> Hesitant
>
> Detached
>
> Unconcerned
>
> Inflexible
>
> Indecisive

Since they represent a large part of the population it would be important for the non-S personalities to bear in mind that these people may be slow starters who like to wait for instructions. However, they are very loyal to their team, and they like to finish what they start.

The "C" personality style:

Words that describe the "C" styles of personality are...

Cautious

Calculating

Contemplative

Criticizing

Conscientious

The C personality is likely to be the deepest thinker of the four types. Seventeen percent of the population has C as their dominant personality trait. They can be accused of analysis paralysis because they want all the facts before making a decision. They have an overwhelming desire to be correct and hate when they are told they are wrong. They make great planners and are very good at finding solutions to problems. They are the most likely personality style to take things personally or to hold a grudge. It is very stressful for them to be in disorganized surroundings or to work with people who are careless or untidy. They also desire to follow procedures and want proof and evidence to make decisions.

C personalities see themselves as...

Conservative

Logical

Alert

Conscientious

Precise

Thorough

Other personality types see Cs as...

Pessimistic

Picky

Fussy

Hard to please

Defensive

Strict

Having a C type of personality on your team can be very valuable. They are the ones that are likely to provide critical analysis and comprehensive problem solving for your project. Because they want quality work and are deadline conscious, they are the ones that keep things on track and make it right. They also tend to be the team members that keep things "real" because they deal with facts.

CAUTION: Your personality is not an excuse for bad character and not an excuse to…

- Be a jerk: "Well this is how I am, so just accept it."

- Be lazy: "I'm just not the ambitious type."

- Be a social misfit: "You know me—I'm just carefree."

Regardless of your personality, you can be successful and of good character. How you succeed and express your character will be influenced by your personality.

Before I go any further, it is important to know two things. First; no one personality is better than another—your personality is perfect for you. Second; no one is 100 percent of any of the four basic types.

We are blends of these types of personalities. Understanding your blend will give you some very good insight into who you really are. Once you understand your personality blend, it will become easier to understand others. No one can employ their GIFT without the aid of others, so understanding how to work with different personalities will make the accomplishment of your purpose easier.

You can determine your basic style by answering a couple of questions. However, I recommend you take an online profile assessment listed in the Resource Section to get a more complete understanding of your particular blend. So here are the basic questions.

You may be more one way than another, depending on the circumstances, and you may be 51% one way and 49% the other, but generally, if no one else is around to influence you, would you say that you are more outgoing or more reserved? If you say you are more outgoing than reserved, then your basic personality style is at the top half of the chart below. If you are more reserved than outgoing, then your basic personality is in the lower half of the chart.

Again, you may be more one way than another, depending on the circumstances, and you may be 51% one way and 49% the other, but generally, if no one else is around to influence you, would you say that you are more task-oriented or more people-oriented? If you are more task-oriented than people-oriented, then your basic personality is on the left side of the chart. If you are more people-oriented than task-oriented, your basic style is on the right side of the chart.

So, for example, if you are an outgoing, task-oriented person, your dominant personality style is that of a D personality. If you are a more reserved, people-oriented person, then you have a dominant personality style of an S personality.

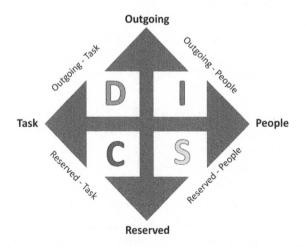

Finding out what your dominant personality style is, and understanding your particular blend of personality, will help you realize how unique you are. It may also explain a few mysteries in your life as well.

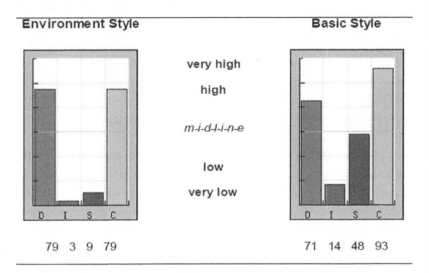

Environment Style		Basic Style

very high

high

m-i-d-l-i-n-e

low

very low

79 3 9 79   71 14 48 93

The chart shows an example of the two graphs which result from taking the DISC personality assessment. In the assessment, you have to choose the word that you think is most like you and the word that is least like you from a set of four words. You must do this several times.

The graph called Environmental Style is the result of your "most like you" answers. It shows how you are likely to respond in your environment: like at work. It shows the behavior that others are most likely to observe. The higher the graph level for each of the four traits, the more that trait is evident in your environment.

The chart above shows a person whose Environmental Style has high C and D traits, and low I and S traits. This would not be a friendly person, and they would be extremely task organized. They would probably appear demanding and cold.

The graph titled Basic Style is the result of your "least like you" answers. This is the real you. When you take the assessment, you will probably find it easy to pick out the words that are least like you, but you might have to think about the words that are most like you. The traits that are higher on the graph are behaviors that feel natural to you. This graph shows characteristics that you tend to demonstrate more consistently.

The Basic Style chart above shows a person that is very detail-oriented (C traits) but doesn't have a problem making decisions (D traits). However, their task orientation is tempered with some I and S traits, the people-oriented characteristics. This person's natural personality is more balanced and friendlier than they are probably acting in their environment at work or at home.

Your Environmental graph might change over time, but your Basic graph will stay constant. The more your Environmental graph matches your Basic graph, the more likely you are in the right environment for your personality.

The graphs show that I, S, and C traits are lower in the Environmental graph than in the Basic graph. This person could be suppressing his detailed personality and his team orientation to appear like more of a decisive leader at work. Over time, that will probably lead to stress and a job change, unless he can begin to behave more like his natural self on the job.

The more you can behave like your natural self, the faster you will be able to work from your strengths.

The more you can behave like your natural self, the faster you will be able to work from your strengths. This is a huge factor in finding your GIFT. If you choose a job or career that requires you to suppress your personality and be something that is not natural for you, even if you become successful at it, you'll find it exhausting and unfulfilling. This is one of the major causes of stress.

If you choose to take the DISC personality assessment (which I would strongly recommend), I would encourage you to pay the most attention to the Basic graph. You should be most interested in who you really are, and not how you may be compensating on a job.

Which brings up another point; even if you have taken a DISC assessment as part of a company program or as part of a human resources requirement for a position, I strongly encourage you to take it again, but this time just for yourself. In the past you may have manipulated your answers on the assessment to give the company what you thought they were looking for. This time you should take the assessment for yourself, answering the questions as truthfully as possible. Your answers should reflect the real you, and not someone you hope to be someday.

As you read the other sections of your DISC assessment, you should focus on all the good things about your personality as opposed to the things you don't like. You should be interested in the things about you that set you apart. I had to learn this the hard way in my own assessment. First, I was a little surprised at the graphs, and the words that best described my personality were not what I considered flattering. The challenge was that they were accurate.

My DISC assessment told me who I was, not who I wanted to be. I could finally ask a pivotal question that changed my life, and could change yours as well: "Okay, God, you made me this way. Why?" When I stopped fighting with how I was created I finally received some good answers. It was not only liberating but profitable. It also enabled me to find my GIFT.

My wife has a very high D personality. When Mary was in the Navy, she was put in charge of a group of senior enlisted personnel who were experts in ship repair and engineering. The group's task was to determine what repairs had to be made on the aircraft carriers home-ported in San Diego. Mary used to brag about never having taken a science or math class in college, and here she was in charge of engineering decisions for many millions of dollars that determined aircraft carrier readiness. Her D personality traits kicked into high gear, and she became so good at getting her personnel to perform that she was recognized as the San Diego Naval Woman of the Year. She loved her job, and her people thought she was an awesome leader.

A D personality who is not using their D traits can be like a ticking time bomb. A friend of mine—I'll call him David—is a high D personality who is literally sick because he is not himself.

David was a very successful leader, but since leaving the military he has been in detail-oriented jobs, trying to please bosses who only think they are leaders. Consequently, David has been incredibly frustrated in most of the positions he has had for the last ten years. While his bosses had trouble making even simple decisions, David can lead and decide quickly but has been relegated to crunching numbers.

David took the personality test and finally understands why he is frustrated and stressed in his career life. He is beginning to understand how he is wired, and that his personality is a GIFT from God designed for him to succeed. David is taking a fresh look at what he wants to do with his life. The true leader in him is beginning to emerge. Now he needs to find a position where he can be in charge, and drive results.

Sometimes, we subconsciously mask our personalities by trying to be people we are not. That is what I did. My parents both loved people and loved being around them—my dad, in particular. He enjoyed going to parties, having a few drinks, and being the life of the party. He loved telling jokes and making people laugh. At family reunions, everyone sought him out for advice, not so much for his sage wisdom, but because they always felt loved by him. Dad could be loud, forceful, and loving all at the same time. He was my hero.

My personality is nothing like his. I much prefer a quiet setting with my best friend, Mary. At a party, I am always looking for an exit. I had to learn how to be sociable and had to cultivate people skills to function in society, but it did not come naturally to me. Since I admired my father so much, I found myself trying to mold my personality into one like his. In college, I went to all the parties, only to be bored. I tried to be one of the boys at work by going out to bars and laughing it up with the guys, only to have my jokes go flat and wonder why I felt out of place. I tried to be a forceful, charismatic leader, but only came off sounding arrogant.

All those missteps came from trying to be something I was not. I don't want to sound like I was a social misfit, because that was not the case, but as soon as I owned up to my real self, and stopped trying to be something I was not, I relaxed around people. Then people relaxed around me.

Since I have personal experience in personality masking, I can recognize that trait in others. It is painful to watch someone cover up who he is and watch him be unaware of what he is doing. Being yourself is much more fun and liberating. It is interesting to note that the one who is masking his true self cannot blame anyone but himself. My father certainly was not trying to mold me into his image. I did that on my own volition.

Marriage relationships and parenting are also greatly affected by personalities. I have spoken with parents who tried to force their personalities on their children. Once they recognized their personalities and the personalities of their children, their parenting changed almost overnight and it became fun again. And even though many marriage challenges are about money, most are about one person not recognizing differences between their personality and that of their spouse.

As you can probably tell, I am a big proponent of you knowing your personality style. It is an important part of finding your GIFT and fulfilling your purpose, and it will probably be a fun learning experience to identify your personality type. I strongly recommend you take the online personality assessment found in the Resource Section and share your results with the person you trust most in life. You will be pleasantly surprised at the discussion your openness will generate.

Father Fracture

This is going to be a touchy subject. What follows is the number one reason that people don't know who they are. It is so emotionally and politically charged that I'll bet you won't hear this anywhere else. I just ask that as you read through it, you don't shoot the messenger.

I once heard a pastor from a large suburban Chicago church talk about something he called a "Father Fracture." A Father Fracture is when you had (or have) a bad relationship (or no relationship) with your father. This will probably lead to having a difficult time having a good relationship (or any relationship, for that matter) with your Father (God).

A Father Fracture can occur when your father didn't live up to his responsibilities. He may have been in the home, but he wasn't there for you. Maybe you never knew your father because he either died when you were young or he might have deserted your family. Maybe you had an abusive father. No matter the situation, it wasn't good. So, how does that make you feel when someone talks about a "father"? Probably not too good.

A Father Fracture is important to recognize because you get your identity from your father. When I say that in person, or to a crowd, it is like dropping a bomb. That's exactly what I thought the first time I heard it. I think most us instinctively know how much our identity is influenced by our fathers, but if you had a bad or absent dad it is kind of hard to swallow.

> # You get your identity from your father.

I was teaching the idea of finding your purpose to a group of law enforcement leaders a while ago, and all was going well...until I got to the subject of the Father Fracture. The room grew quiet and faces changed. Some looked inquisitive, like I sparked their interest, while others withdrew.

After the training, several of the seasoned cops came up to me privately. They each mentioned that they thought what I said was true, even if it picked a few scabs. What they wanted to know was if I could prove it. Was there evidence that the Father Fracture was real and that one's identity comes from the father? They were interested for themselves, but they intuitively understood how this idea affected the populations they dealt with daily. Well, it turns out there is plenty of evidence, and it is a huge problem that is only getting worse. The challenge is that no one wants to touch this problem with a ten-foot pole.

David Blankenhorn wrote *Fatherless America* in 1995. His research and references on the subject are very thorough. Since the book was published the problems he described have only gotten worse. So, for those of you who like to see the facts, here are some of the issues and statistics found by David (I have updated the numbers based on the most recent sources available):

One of the things I found remarkable is that until the mid-1800s it was the father, not the mother, that had the primary responsibility for child training, religious and moral education, and societal guidance. It was industrialization that caused the change. Once fathers had to go to work in a factory and be away from the family all day, these roles shifted to mothers.

Fatherlessness is the leading cause of poverty in America.

Fatherlessness is the leading cause of poverty in America. In 2014, 23.6% of children lived in father-absent homes, according to the US Census Bureau. Fifty-percent of all children will live in a single-parent home at some time before they reach age eighteen. In 2012, 41% of US children were born to never-married parents, according to the National Center for Health Statistics. Blankenhorn says that half of all children living with a single mother are in poverty, which is five times higher than children living with both parents.

The effects of fatherlessness can be devastating. For instance, child abuse is more likely to occur in single-parent homes than when both parents are there. There is also a greater risk of drug abuse, alcohol abuse, mental illness, suicide, and poor educational performance. In women, there is an increase in promiscuity and teenage pregnancy, and in men, there is increased violence and criminality.

I recently had a dream that related to the effects of fatherlessness. In my dream, I saw the word *feckless* as part of the title of a book. The title was on a blue banner with the stars and stripes of the American flag as the background. The sense I had of the dream was that America had become a *feckless* nation.

To be honest, I did not know what the word *feckless* meant, so I had to look it up. A feckless person is weak, ineffective, lacking purpose, and irresponsible. In this sense, irresponsible means a person who is not answerable to a higher authority. All of these traits can be directly attributed to growing up without a father. A person with a good father who loved you unconditionally would probably not be feckless.

Involved fathers seem to have a special influence on the development of empathy in children. They stress things like competition, challenge, initiative, risk-taking, and independence. Mothers, on the other hand, are the caretakers. They stress personal safety and emotional security.

I think you can see that both mothers and fathers are necessary for the development of children. To diminish the role of either fathers or mothers would be a mistake, one that we seem to be making these days. If you didn't receive the unconditional love that your father was supposed to give you, you would have no example by which to fully recognize the unconditional love your Father has for you. Unfortunately, that describes more and more children and young adults.

Hollywood movies often mirror what is happening in society. Some of my favorite movies are *Gladiator*, *The Kingdom of Heaven*, the *Star Wars* movies, and the *Lord of the Rings* trilogy. All of these have huge Father Fractures as part of their themes. My wife, Mary, likes the romantic "chick flicks," and almost all of them have Father Fractures running through their plots. It seems that Hollywood may be telling us something.

Many people I speak with today grew up in single-parent families and consider their single-parent families as "normal." Other people said they were fortunate to have their father in the home when they grew up, even though their dad was rarely ever there. If that describes your dad, did he help you, guide you, and provide leadership in your family? Or did your mom do those things? The point is that even families with two parents often have a dad who is absent for the children. Does any of this relate to you?

David, from the earlier example about personality, has a Father Fracture. David assumed he and his father had a great relationship. When I asked him how often his father told him he loved him, or that he was proud of him, David said "never." He said he didn't have "that kind of a relationship" with his father. That statement baffled me. What kind of relationship did he think he was supposed to have?

The more I checked into this question, the more I realized most men and women don't know what a proper relationship with their father is supposed to look like. That is because they have never seen one.

> # Most people don't know what a proper relationship with their father is supposed to look like.

I asked my wife about this and was surprised by her answer. Her dad died when she was a teenager. Before his passing, he and Mary's mother were separated. There was major tension in their home and a lot of stress and alcohol abuse. So, when I asked Mary what she thought a good relationship with a father should look like, she told me she saw it in my father. She told me how awesome it was for her to see my mother sitting on my father's lap the first time she came over to our home. Having grown up in a home with a strong and loving father, I took it for granted. My late dad was by no means perfect, but he is still the best example I know for what a father is supposed to be.

The interesting thing about my dad is that he had a huge Father Fracture of his own. As a teenager, he left home after his tenth-grade year and joined the Marine Corps. The year was 1939, and since the US had not yet entered World War II, he didn't join the Marines out of patriotic fervor. He just wanted to get out of his home situation. Apparently, his father had not gotten along too well with his mother, and his father had a bad habit of spending his paycheck on drinking and "playing the ponies." As the middle of six kids in a rough neighborhood in Philadelphia, my father needed to escape.

By the time I came along, Dad had fought in World War II and Korea. He was the picture of the perfect Marine First Sergeant; he had a booming command voice and all the medals to go with it. If he looked into your eyes, you would swear he could see right into your soul. It was impossible to lie to him.

This same tough, rugged, highly respected man tucked my sister and me into bed every night. Before we were tucked in, my mom, my sister, my dad, and I would all kneel by our beds to say prayers. Every night Dad would ask me if I was warm enough, and then he'd kiss me before he left the room. I never once had to guess if I was loved by my parents.

As I grew, Dad was always there for me. I remember, as a teenager, agreeing to take another guy's Sunday morning paper route for him while he went on vacation. At 4 a.m. on a Sunday morning, I waited on a corner a block away from our house for newspapers to be dropped off. It was dark, I had no flashlight, and rain began to fall. I had no idea what I was doing. I walked home with the papers and sat in the kitchen, crying as I started to wrap the newspapers in plastic.

I didn't want to wake Dad up, because I wanted him to be proud of me, not see me looking like a basket case. Dad must have heard me because he dressed and came downstairs. He never complained about the time or told me how stupid I was; he just helped me deliver the papers. When we were done, he put his arm around me and then went back to bed. Needless to say, I didn't last as a paperboy.

David did not have those kinds of experiences with his father; neither did my wife. Only after hearing the pastor in Chicago speak about the Father Fracture did I realize how truly blessed I was to have grown up with a real father. No matter what I did, or did not do, my father always told me how proud he was of me and that he loved me. He gave me my identity as an approved son of a great man.

I fully realize that some of you who are reading this had a father as good as mine, or better. But most of you did not. Realizing that you have a Father Fracture is 90% of the battle. Until you deal with it, you will not have a firm foundation from which to move forward.

The following are some telltale signs that you have a Father Fracture. (Please note that any one of them could be devastating to you and could leave scars that interfere with knowing your real self. Please also note that I am not making any judgmental statements about your situation.)

> You never knew your father
>
> Your father abandoned your family
>
> Your father died when you were young
>
> Your father was in the home but not there for you
>
> Your father never, or rarely, told you he loved you
>
> You felt that you had to earn his approval
>
> You felt that you had to earn his love
>
> Your father never corrected you
>
> Your mother did not respect your father
>
> You had feelings of insecurity as a child
>
> You were physically or emotionally abused
>
> You are promiscuous now
>
> You have gender issues
>
> You are angry at the world

When you have had the approval of your father, without having had to earn it, you have a source of confidence that lasts a lifetime. When you KNOW you are loved by your father, no matter what you do or don't do, the natural result is to want to please him. You won't need anyone else's approval to make you feel complete.

Having your dad tell you he is proud of you, and that his pride is not coming from your performance, instills a sense of pride in you that no one can remove. For whatever reason, these things are more important and have a greater effect on you when they come from your father than from your mother. Somehow, mothers are expected to have these feelings and say these things to their children, and it is vitally important to us to have them from our mothers. But if a person doesn't get them from their father, a very important piece of their identity is missing.

Ultimately, a good father has one crucial task. By being a good father—one who loves, approves, protects, provides for, teaches, and guides his children—a father teaches his children about the nature of God. Unfortunately, the fathers of today's society have not done a very good job.

For most of society, the word *father* does not conjure up any of the attributes it should but often is a bad word. *Father* often makes people feel neglected, abandoned, or abused. It is no wonder that people are leaving mainline denominations. Who would want to belong to a religion that calls God the Father when they have no idea how good He really is?

> # For most of today's society, *father* is a bad word!

Healing a Father Fracture has two parts. First, recognizing you have one. You can't fix what you don't know, or won't admit, is broken. If your father did not give you unconditional love, made you work for it, or wasn't there for you, that's not your fault. He did not fulfill his role in helping you form your identity. Second, finding out for yourself (yes, it is up to you, and no one else can do this for you) that your Father (capital F) really does love you, approve of you, protects you, provides for you, teaches you, and guides you. He's the one who gave you your personality, your GIFT, and your purpose. He chose these things specifically for you because He wants more for you than you want for yourself. Even if your father blew it, your Father doesn't.

Generation

Just like your personality and the Father Fracture, who you are is influenced by your generation.

Because we are living longer, we now have four very different generations in the workforce all at the same time. The benefit is that we have four generational perspectives on the challenges of today. The problem is that we have four generational perspectives on the challenges of today. Depending on your generation, you could be excited or depressed.

Let's start by defining the different generations. They are:

1. Traditional—after the "Greatest Generation (WWII)" but before Baby Boomers. Only a few of this generation are still working

2. Baby Boomers

3. Gen X—also called latchkey kids

4. Millennials—also called Gen Y and net Gen

Each generation has major differences in how they act, communicate, and think. The following chart helps to define some of those for the three dominant generations in the workforce.

Baby Boomer (75 million)	Gen X (66 million)	Gen Y / net Gen / Millennial (largest generation)
Born 1945-1964	Born 1964-1982	Graduate HS in 2000
Industrial Age	Transition Era	Information Age
Traditional	Independent	Work in Groups
Optimistic about Future	"Whatever"	Pessimistic about Future
Call	Email	TXT

The Baby Boomer generation is a huge population, roughly seventy-five million. They were born between 1945 and 1964. They grew up in the Industrial Age—a time before computers and cell phones. Most of today's management theory is still based on Baby Boomers' thinking, which values the bottom line and believes workers are numbers that can be replaced. If you've ever been told to do something "because I said so" or because "that's how we've always done it," chances are you are hearing it from an Industrial Age Baby Boomer. They still represent a large number of business owners and corporate managers.

Baby Boomers are known for their more traditional values. When they were growing up the assault on fatherhood hadn't fully hit. They expected to do better than their parents and were told the key to getting ahead was more education. Their preferred method of communicating is either face to face or on the phone. They grew up with TV shows like *Gunsmoke*, *Leave It to Beaver*, and *The Andy Griffith Show*.

Generation X is a kind of transition generation. They were caught in-between the Industrial Age and the Information Age. They weren't born in a world with computers and the internet, but they learned to use them as tools. Their generation numbers about sixty-six million and they were born between 1964 and 1982.

Generation X was taught to be independent. Their Baby Boomer parents were so engaged in their careers that many Gen Xers were left to take care of themselves. That is how they got the nickname "latchkey kids." It comes from the fact that many in this generation had their own house key because they needed it to unlock the door when they got home from school since both parents were still at work. They didn't have parents hovering over their every move, so they became very independent.

If there is a word that described a person from Generation X it would be "whatever" and they are not as driven to succeed as their predecessors. Their favorite mode of communication is email, but they have adapted to texting and social media. They are not as optimistic as the Baby Boomer generation, preferring to go with the flow. They grew up watching *Friends* and *Seinfeld* on TV.

The Millennial generation is projected to surpass the huge Baby Boom generation as the nation's largest living generation, according to population projections released by the US. Census Bureau. They were born after 1982 and grew up with computers and the web. They were also schooled differently than the previous generation, being taught to work in groups to gather information for projects.

Their expectations are remarkably different from previous generations. They expect to do worse economically than their parents, but they expect a job to come with a college degree. They also tend to communicate via social media and texting rather than have social interaction face to face or on the phone.

According to the Brookings Institute, Millennials:

- will comprise more than one in three adult Americans by 2020

- will make up as much as 75% of the US workforce by 2025

- already account for more than $1 trillion in US consumer spending

- would rather make $40,000/year at a job they love than $100,000/year at a job they think is boring

On a flight from Chicago to Washington, DC, I was seated between two young Millennial women. I had just read an article in *USA Today* (it was a courtesy copy) about the attitudes and work ethic of the Millennial generation. The cover story picture showed a young woman in casual attire and flip-flops sitting on top of a desk in an office room. Not exactly the traditional work environment I am used to. So, I asked my two Millennial seat-mates what they thought of the article. They immediately conferred with each other (they were total strangers) and then told me they agreed with what the author of the article had said about the way Millennials work compared to previous generations.

All of a sudden, the oxygen masks popped out of the ceilings over our seats. My first thought was, *Wow, that's unusual.* To my great surprise, no one screamed or acted crazy. The pilot came on the loudspeaker and said we had lost cabin pressure but there was nothing else wrong with the airplane. We ended up making a precautionary landing in Cincinnati. This meant I had more time to interrogate the two women I sat with. It was very educational.

When I finally returned to my office in Chicago, I gathered all the Millennials in the office to ask their opinion of the *USA Today* article. I told them what the two women on the airplane said and asked if they agreed. The conversation soon became loud and excited. They couldn't believe how I thought, and they were amazed a Baby Boomer listened to them. The conversation centered around "why."

Almost every time I would ask one of them to do something they would ask, "Why?" To my way of thinking this was insubordinate and just being stubborn. What I didn't realize was why they were asking "why." Millennials are part of the Information Age. Through computers, the internet, cell phones, and a host of other technology they are used to gathering all the pertinent information they can before beginning a project. When they are asking "why" it is so that they can gather the correct information. I learned this from my two Millennial flying companions and was eager to see if my co-workers thought the same way.

As the discussion in our office progressed the CEO came storming out of his office and we all thought he was angry. Well, he was certainly emotional, but he wasn't angry with any of us. It was because he recently had been "challenged" by his son with a "why" question. Overhearing our conversation, the CEO now understood that his son's "challenge" wasn't a challenge at all. Everyone had a good laugh, and the communication in that office rose to a new level.

What's the point? The point is that your generation is a part of who you are. It affects how you think and how you choose to communicate. To a large extent, it determines your assumptions regarding history, values, current events, politics, and religion. For instance, many Millennials don't know who Ronald Reagan was or who Bill Clinton is (other than Hillary's husband), and they don't care. Until the last few years they had not experienced a growing, prosperous economy so they are unsure about their economic future.

One last note about Millennials. Many Baby Boomers and Gen X people think the work ethic of Millennials is below par. They also think Millennials are narcissistic; a "me" generation. I have to admit I fell into that trap as well...until I talked to a friend who was a Marine Corps general. His opinion is that this generation has produced some of the finest Marines he has ever seen. Their ingenuity and resourcefulness are amazing. He said the difference is that they must be led, not managed.

I'll get into the differences between leadership and management later in the book, but you can't just demand performance from Millennials. They need to be led. I think that is because many of them have not experienced a good father relationship or leadership in their lives, but they respond to it exceptionally well when they experience it.

Gender

This is not as touchy a subject as you might assume. (Remember, the point of this book is to help you realize you have a Special GIFT.)

Hopefully, you have already come to realize that how you think is affected by your particular personality and that everyone doesn't think like you. In addition to your personality, your gender affects how you think as well.

> Did you know that scientists have discovered one hundred differences between the male and female brain?

Did you know that scientists have discovered one hundred differences between the male and female brain? I learned this from a *Psychology Today* article published by Gregory L. Jantz, Ph.D. Men have seven times more gray matter than women, and have information and action processing centers in specific boxes in a specific area of the brain. Men can have tunnel vision when they are doing something, so once they are concentrating on a task or game, they probably won't show too much sensitivity to other people or even be aware of their surroundings. (I can hear you ladies laughing in agreement.)

On the other hand, women have ten times more white matter than their male counterparts. White matter is the networking grid that connects the brain's gray matter and other processing centers with one another. It is the reason girls tend to transition more quickly between tasks than boys. It is also the reason why females are great multitaskers, while men excel in highly task-focused projects.

When I listen to two women talking I'm amazed at how they can follow each other. Shifting a conversation from one subject to another and then back again is natural to them. That's because everything is connected to everything else in the female brain. I often have to stop my wife in midsentence and ask her if we just changed subjects. Her reply is usually something pithy like, "Just keep up."

Females have verbal centers on both sides of the brain while males only have verbal centers on the left hemisphere. There are also chemical differences that make men tend to be less inclined to sit still for as long as females, and makes them tend to be more physically impulsive and aggressive than women.

Guys, here is a warning: If your best girl says she wants to talk about a problem, she probably isn't looking for you to solve it for her. She probably just wants to talk. I know it doesn't make sense to you, but it does to her...doesn't it, ladies? She'll let you know if she needs your help.

So, while it might not be politically correct, when it comes to who you are, scientifically speaking, your gender does make a difference. Of course, most of you already knew that even if you didn't know the science behind it.

How You Think About Money

Before I even start, some of you have different reactions to the word *money*. To some, it represents what they want. If they got honest with themselves, they are a whole lot more interested in having more money than finding their purpose.

To others money is evil, and they think they shouldn't want it...even though they really do. Somewhere along the line, they were taught that money is the root of evil and it is just greedy to want more of the stuff. Actually, the verse goes like this: "The love of money is the root of all evil." If you love money more than people or God, you have a problem, but to want to have a better life is normal.

How you think about money is a function of your assumptions and the way you were taught, your gender, and a predisposition based on your purpose. Do you assume that money is scarce, that it's all in the hands of the rich? Or do you assume there is enough money to go around for anyone that wants to earn it? Those are assumptions, but what are the facts?

> ## "The number one thing Americans want
> ## is more money."
> ### Frank Luntz

According to *What Americans Really Want, Really* by Frank Luntz, the research shows that the number one thing Americans want is more money. However, why they want it is different for men than it is for women. He says that his research shows that men want more money to have more freedom. They also want it for more toys...so they can enjoy their freedom. It's the adage of he who dies with the most stuff wins.

Women, on the other hand, also want more money. Their reasons have more to do with personal security and to alleviate financial fear. With the rise of fatherlessness in America and a trend where males seem to be abdicating their traditional roles as men, more women are taking their financial security into their own hands.

Lastly, we are predisposed to think about money in one of three ways. You may be naturally wired to think in terms of security, comfort, or wealth when it comes to your money. Your predisposition to one of these ways of thinking can be heavily influenced by several factors, the major one being your personality. Let me explain:

Security—A predisposition to thinking in terms of security means you don't like risk. If that's you, you probably want a secure job, in an established company, that has good benefits. Safe investments that can get you the American dream in a nice neighborhood sounds good to you. In addition to almost all women, security is what appeals to the S personalities we described earlier. Since about half the population is women and 69% of the total population has the S personality as a top trait, then you can see why most people think in terms of security when it comes to money. Politicians and advertisers know this as well, and that is where almost all their efforts are targeted.

Comfort—People who are predisposed to think about money in terms of comfort are prone to taking significantly more risk. They see money as a means to increase their comfort in life. To one person money for comfort means working overtime or a second job to get a bigger TV and a nicer La-Z-Boy. To another person, it means taking a high-risk (in the eyes of the security person), commission-only job so they can have a nice beach house in addition to their residence.

These are the people we would normally call "rich." They make a lot of money, and they spend a lot of money. Many of the "Comfort" people have a high D or I personality. The D-I or I-D styles are usually outspoken, people oriented, and driven. They make the best salespeople and often occupy CEO positions. A friend of mine in the Marine Corps used to tell me, "If you have money in the bank and vacation time on the books you aren't living right." He became a successful partner in a large brokerage firm in Manhattan. Go figure!

Wealth—People who think in terms of wealth exercise delayed gratification, take calculated risks, and have a plan for their money. Often a wealth-oriented person may live right next door to you, and you'd never know it until they moved into their new mansion they bought with cash. Many people would like to be rich, but very few are oriented and plan to be wealthy. A wealthy person can come from any of the personality traits, but they probably have at least some degree of C in their blend. It takes planning and restraint to become wealthy, and those are C-like traits.

How you think about money is part of who you are. Even if you are predisposed to security, it doesn't mean you can't have comfort or wealth. It just means you think about security first. One way of thinking is not better or worse than another, but how you think about money will be a factor in your purpose. If your purpose is to make a difference for the entire planet, then you will probably need large sums of money to make that happen. If your purpose is to be an influence in your community, then the amount of money you will need may not be as large. I think you get the point.

How You Give and Receive Love

In his book *The Five Love Languages*, Gary Chapman tells us that we don't all give or receive love the same way. When I first read his book, I was amazed. I didn't think there was anything new that I could discover about my wife or our marriage. Obviously, that wasn't true, because I learned about her personality and strengths after about twenty years of being married to her. So, discovering that we gave and received love differently shouldn't have been a surprise. But it was.

Just like your personality and the other factors that combine to make you so unique, your way of loving is unique. Gary Chapman boils love languages down to five different types, but just as with the four major types of personalities, each person is a blend. He says that we primarily love in one of these five ways:

- by giving and receiving gifts

- by acts of service

- by spending quality time

- by physical touch, or

- by words of affirmation

If someone gives you a gift, no matter how small or large the gift, and that makes you feel special and loved, then your love language may be giving and receiving gifts. If someone doing things for you makes you feel especially appreciated, then acts of service may be your love language. When just being in the same room, doing nothing in particular, or being together on a road trip makes you feel special, then quality time is your love language. If holding hands, a back rub, or a head massage tells you that, no matter what else is going on, he still loves you, then physical touch may be your love language. If your heart warms when she tells you how much she appreciates you, and that you are great in her eyes, then your love language may be words of affirmation.

One language is not better than another, and you may have a couple of languages that stand out for you, but one will be your dominant language. It is important to remember that just because you receive love in a certain way does not necessarily mean that the one you love receives love in the same way. That would be rare. So, not only do you need to be aware of your language, but you need to be able to speak the language of the one you love.

I am laughing inside as I think of the mistakes I have made with Mary in this area. When we were newly married, we lived in Encinitas, California. Florists from all over the country purchased the beautiful flowers that grew on the hills in Encinitas. On any backroad around Encinitas, you could find flower stands selling beautiful bouquets of locally grown flowers at really good prices.

Being the loving husband, and trying to show my new wife how much I thought of her, I would frequently stop at a flower stand and buy an arrangement, then put it in a vase on our dining room table for her. Now, I should tell you I am not a flower guy, and giving or receiving gifts is not my love language. I was doing this for Mary because I had seen in movies and on TV that girls like this kind of stuff.

Several days went by and not a peep from Mary. I finally mustered the courage to bring it up to my new bride. I asked her if she liked the flowers. Her response was, "Oh my goodness, I didn't even see them. Those are nice. Thank you." That was it! So, I did a very intelligent thing. I didn't get offended but asked her if gifts or flowers did anything for her. She liked flowers, but only if she grew them in her garden. As far as gifts went, they were certainly appreciated, but she did not need them to tell her I loved her. I am a lucky man!

I discovered her love language by accident. We had an awesome Italian restaurant close to where we lived, and Friday night pizza was a ritual for me. We would often find ourselves at Papachino's restaurant in Del Mar, waiting for a table on Friday nights. Usually, Mary would be exhausted from the week's work, and she would put her legs up on my lap as we waited. One Friday I started giving her a foot massage, and I think she went to heaven. She kept saying, "Oh, that feels so good," over and over.

One of the waitresses overheard her and looked right at me. She asked, "Do you have a brother?" I guess the waitress's love language was physical touch, as was Mary's. Notice, I didn't say groping or having sex when I said physical touch. To this day, no matter how tense things might be between us, if I scratch her back or her head before we go to sleep, Mary knows I still love her and that everything is good between us.

I have a good friend who likes massages, so he has a habit of giving people shoulder massages as a form of greeting. Many people like it, but I am not one of them. I finally had to tell him I loved him like a brother, but if he ever tried to give me another shoulder massage, I was going to break his hands. Physical touch is NOT my love language. For me to give love in this way to my wife is an effort, but I know how much it means to her, so I am happy to give her love in the form she needs.

Even though I sort of knew her love language after years of being together, it wasn't confirmed until we read *The Five Love Languages*. Mary wasn't sure of my language until she read the book and we had a chance to discuss it together. I'm one of those people who like order, and I am visually oriented. Seeing things out of place in our home, or seeing our home become dirty, really bothers me. Mary often doesn't even notice the things that bug me. Remember, she didn't see the flowers either. So, to keep a sense of order in our home, I started picking up and doing a lot of the cleaning in our house.

She told me she thought I was doing this as an act of service for her, which is not her love language, nor mine. I finally had to set her straight. I wasn't doing those things for her; I was doing them for me. If she did them, I would appreciate it, but I would just like the sense of order, not the idea that she was doing something for me. What I love is just spending time together. Whether watching a movie together on the couch, riding bikes, or exploring someplace new, just knowing she wants to be with me is what makes me feel loved.

It is sad, but we have all heard the stories of couples who have been married for a long time and then divorce. Sometimes, they hang on until their children leave the nest, or sometimes they are in their sixties and just can't stay together any longer. There is a story in *The Five Love Languages* about a couple like this. The man reached the end of his rope but agreed to get some marriage counseling before they called it quits. In counseling, he said that he just couldn't please her. He did this for her, and he did that for her, and she never appreciated him for it. Obviously, his love language was acts of service.

His wife, on the other hand, told him that all she ever wanted was to spend time with him. Sitting on the couch together, or watching TV or a movie would have meant the world to her, but he was always too busy fixing the cars or doing this or that. This couple had been together for over forty years, and neither of them knew how they needed to receive love.

How do you give and receive love? Don't you think it would be a good idea to know this about yourself? Fortunately, several tools can aid you in figuring it out. In the Resource Section, you will find a link to the *Five Love Languages Quiz.* If you are married or are thinking of being married, I would recommend you have the other person take the quiz also. It should be revealing, and it could save you a lot of heartaches.

There is another aspect of giving love that is important. As a D and C personality blend, my personality profile has described me as being cold, critical, and aloof—not exactly words that I would regard as being praiseworthy, nor are they very loving. It took me a while to accept that those words were pretty accurate.

I wanted, and prayed for, help in becoming more loving and compassionate towards people. The problem was I was not wired that way, and being loving and compassionate was real effort and unnatural for me. Then I discovered something that resolved my dilemma. Until I got okay with who I really was, there was no way I would discover my GIFT.

Once I discovered my GIFT, and then began to develop it and give it away, I learned how I was meant to be compassionate and loving. Now, in the process of using my GIFT, my compassion, patience, and love flow without effort. The more I use my GIFT, the more these virtues became evident. So, if you are having a difficult time being the loving person you want to be, my advice would be to first get good with who you are—then discover your GIFT.

The Real You

I mentioned earlier that there are numerous facets to who you are. You are a complex, one-of-a-kind person. The six things we talked about here are:

1. Your personality

2. Your father

3. Your generation

4. Your gender

5. Your thoughts about money

6. How you give and receive love

I strongly encourage you to take the personality assessment (found in the Resource Section) to find out your particular blend of the four major styles, the D, I, S, and C. Understanding your personality helps you to realize that you have a special way of responding to the world around you—your natural behavior. You were born that way and it is perfect for you. Going with your personality, rather than trying to change it, will help you to discover your purpose and to make a difference.

If the only thing you get from this book is a better understanding of who you are, I think you will have found a priceless asset. But, since the subject of this book is your Special GIFT, who you really are is just a step in the process. The six factors of the real you that we just discussed are a vital part of the unique way you will make a difference.

Chapter 6
Your Special GIFT

Having a Special GIFT is just not a normal topic of conversation. I've never heard people talk about their Special GIFT in a locker room or at work. I've certainly not heard anyone talk about GIFT on TV. We don't talk about GIFT at family gatherings (well, I do, but you probably don't). A pastor might talk about having a gift in a sermon, but it usually ends there. And you might hear a motivational speaker talk about possessing a gift, but how many people go to motivational speeches?

What Your Special GIFT Is Not

In teaching the seven steps outlined in *The Joe Purpose Master Key* (the "how-to" book I mentioned earlier), I found some confusion on the part of some as to what their Special GIFT actually is. Most of the confusion came from those who did not take the recommended assessments. But to be as clear as possible, and to eliminate any confusion, here is what your Special GIFT is **not**:

- **A present you receive at Christmas**

  I realize that Joe Purpose is holding a present in his hand on the book cover, but that was just to get your attention. Your Special GIFT is not a physical thing that you receive or give to someone.

- **Personality**

  As you discovered in Chapter 5, your personality is a very important component of who you are. There are many valuable lessons you can take away from learning your true personality, but your personality is not your GIFT. Personality determines your behavior, while your GIFT is much more.

- **Something you make up**

  Most people do not know their Special GIFT, at least not as I define it. When I ask someone if they know their GIFT, a natural response is to tell me what they think it might be. My wife and I are fond of saying that when people don't know the truth they MSU. That stands for Make Stuff Up.

- **Something you choose**

  You can't just pick a GIFT out of a hat and claim it for yourself. Neither can you copy someone else's GIFT. You are born with your GIFT and it is unique to you. You can, and should, choose to develop it and to employ it.

- **Someone else's responsibility to find it for you**

  Your GIFT belongs to you and it is your responsibility to discover it. No matter how well someone else may know you, or how accurate an assessment may be, only you know how you think.

- **Something you keep to yourself**

  You may have heard the phrase "No man is an island." Well, it is true. Your GIFT is meant to be given, which is why it has value. Other people's GIFTs will need to be combined with yours for their GIFT to have the greatest effect. You will also need to use the GIFTs of others for your GIFT to shine.

- **Better than someone else's**

  No one's GIFT is better than another. Your GIFT is unique to you and fits just where it should. You can be a great you, but only a mediocre someone else.

What Your Special GIFT Is

In a word, it is what makes you **unique**. Your Special GIFT is:

- **Your unique God-given way of thinking**

    No two minds think the same way. Your way of thinking is by design and for a reason. It was specifically created for you. So, you are not weird...you are GIFTed.

- **The one talent you can develop into greatness**

    The talent I am speaking of is not the physical but the mental part of your talent. For instance, an athlete may have superior physical attributes, but only when those attributes are married with drive and determination would we say he or she is GIFTed. There is something that you think about better than anyone else. We may observe it as "talent," but it is much more than that. It is your Special GIFT.

- **The way God designed you to succeed in life**

    How you make a difference is by operating in your Special GIFT. If you have ever heard someone talk about a time when they were in "their zone," they were probably talking about operating in their GIFT. People can't rock your boat, and usually don't even try, when you operate in your GIFT because you are so confident about what you are doing. That special and unique way of thinking is what you were given in order to succeed in life.

- **The way you were designed to show love**

    Employing your Special GIFT is a joy, it makes you feel at peace, and it gives you exceptional patience with people. Operating in your Special GIFT benefits others in a way that can only be called love. If you have ever struggled with the impossibility of loving others as yourself it is because you were trying to make yourself do something you thought was right. When you give your Special GIFT loving others happens naturally, almost without effort.

Why Don't People Know They Have a Special GIFT?

Finding out who you are can be kind of fun, especially if you do it in a group. But for some reason, the idea of having a GIFT and finding your purpose intimidates many people. Very few people ever seek their purpose, and some go out of their way to avoid it.

> ## As a reminder, your purpose is to employ your Special GIFT.

As a reminder, your purpose is to employ your Special GIFT. So, if you want to find your purpose and get all its benefits, you'll need to find your GIFT first.

If having a Special GIFT can do so much for you, and if it is the key to operating in the Second System I described earlier, then why don't people know their Special GIFT? That's a good question, isn't it?

There are several answers. Here are a few:

- No one talks about GIFT
- They aren't looking for it
- They are too busy just trying to make ends meet
- They are ingrained in the First System
- They are doing okay compared to others
- They don't know who they are

- They don't know where to begin

- They are afraid to find out

- It involves thinking

No One Talks About GIFT

Your Special GIFT is just not a topic of conversation. As already mentioned, I've never heard people talk about GIFT in a locker room, at work, or at family gatherings.

They Aren't Looking for It

If they don't know they have a Special GIFT, then why would they even look for it? No one ever told me I had a Special GIFT, and I certainly wasn't looking for it. I only tripped over it when I tried to find out why I wasn't passionate about anything.

They Are Too Busy Just Trying to Make Ends Meet

They could be stuck in a survival mode just trying to keep their heads above water financially. Having been there, I know how difficult it is to find a way out.

They Are Ingrained in the First System

Most people don't know they are in a system, let alone that they have a choice between two opposing systems. If all you have ever been taught is go to school, get good grades so you can get into a good college, so you can get a good job, so you can work hard for forty or fifty years, so you can retire—and here's the kicker—and you think this will work for you, then why do you need a Special GIFT? There is a better way that involves employing your Special GIFT so you can succeed in life. Struggle does not have to define your existence.

They Are Doing Okay Compared to Others

They look around at their family, their friends, and their co-workers and figure, "I'm doing okay compared to them." The only person you should compare yourself to is you. You have a purpose and a reason for being here, and your purpose is not the same as theirs. By the way, they wish they had a purpose, so why would you want their lives?

They Don't Know Who They Are

The biggest reason people don't know their GIFT and aren't looking for it is that they don't know who they are. If your starting point is a false image of the real you, you cannot find your GIFT.

They Don't Know Where to Begin

I find that many "experts" who talk about purpose just jump right in, lumping everyone into the same group. You have to start with who you really are. Your purpose will be unique and so will your starting point.

They Are Afraid to Find Out

They are afraid their GIFT may not be what they want, or maybe it might interfere with the way things are now. And what will their friends think?

It Involves Thinking

Your Special GIFT is your very unique way of thinking. That is what separates you from everybody else who has ever lived.

In the introduction to Napoleon Hill's famous book on success, *Think and Grow Rich*, he writes, *"In every chapter of this book, mention is made of the money-making secret which has made fortunes for hundreds of exceedingly wealthy men whom I have carefully analyzed over a long period of years."*

The exceedingly wealthy men he refers to are Henry Ford, William Wrigley Jr, John Wanamaker, George Eastman, Charles Schwab, Theodore Roosevelt, William Jennings Bryan, Thomas Edison, and many more. If these people knew a secret about making money, and it was revealed in a book, wouldn't you want to know what it is? And yet countless people have read *Think and Grow Rich* without discovering the secret. I'll give you a hint—the secret is on the cover!

The secret that the wealthy have discovered is how to think. You have to Think to Grow Rich. But what does it mean to think? Doesn't everybody think? Apparently not. According to Thomas Edison, *"Five percent of the people think; ten percent of the people think they think, and the other eighty-five percent would rather die than think."*

The more I dug into the idea that most people don't really think, I began to ask a logical question: Why don't they? Here is what some famous people had to say on that subject.

"Thinking is the hardest work there is, which is probably the reason so few engage in it."

— **Henry Ford**

"Simple can be harder than complex: You have to work hard to get your thinking clean to make it simple. But it's worth it in the end because once you get there, you can move mountains."

— **Steve Jobs**

"People don't like to think. If one thinks, one must reach conclusions. Conclusions are not always pleasant."

— **Helen Keller**

"I insist on a lot of time being spent, almost every day, to just sit and think. That is very uncommon in American business. I read and think. So, I do more reading and thinking and make fewer impulse decisions than most people in business. I do it because I like this kind of life."

— **Warren Buffett**

What Does It Mean to think?

With those quotes in mind, what does it mean to think? You might say that is a silly question, but the reality is that most people use their feelings and emotions rather than thinking things through. Feelings and emotions are mental reactions or sensations based on perception or unreasoned opinion. People who "think" with their emotions or feelings don't originate thoughts or use reason; they merely react to things. This kind of "thinking" can be emotionally exhausting but it doesn't take any effort.

Thought, on the other hand, is a developed intention or plan that engages reasoning power and the power to imagine or conceive. Thinking means that you reflect or ponder in your mind, that you form a mental picture or exercise the powers of judgment, conception, or reason. It requires imagination and effort.

"First comes thought; then organization of that thought, into ideas and plans; then transformation of those plans into reality. The beginning, as you will observe, is in your imagination."

— *Napoleon Hill*

The First Step in Finding Your GIFT

The first step in finding your gift is overcoming inertia.

Inertia is a tendency to do nothing or to remain unchanged. It can also be defined as the property by which something continues in its existing state of rest or uniform motion in a straight line unless that state is changed by an external force.

This is a fancy way of saying that it takes effort to change.

Whether you are doing nothing at all or you're going warp speed in the wrong direction, something has to break you free of the inertia that's keeping you stuck where you are. Just the fact that you are already reading this means you are in the process of overcoming inertia.

You have a seed of greatness in you. Notice that was a statement, not a question. It is a fact that you have a Special GIFT. When your GIFT is developed, you will find that some people will call you a genius. But don't get too stuck on yourself; everyone has a GIFT.

If you knew you had a Special GIFT, and it could take you as far as you wanted to go in life, wouldn't you want to know what it is? Yet the fear of discovering just how great you are can be overwhelming to many. It is much easier to go through life without knowing how great you can be. Then, no one will expect anything of you, including yourself. Ultimately, I guess you could call this the fear of success.

The word *greatness* throws some people. As soon as you tell them they could be great at something their negative self-talk kicks in, telling them they could never be great at anything. They feel inadequate because either they failed at something or someone told them they were inadequate—a loser.

Almost everyone feels inadequate, somehow. Don't you? I have had many more people tell me what I couldn't do than what I could do. As I mentioned earlier, I once had a dream to play professional baseball. The problem was my fastball wasn't all that fast and sometimes my curveball didn't curve. I felt inadequate, and no one argued with me.

Some people don't try to be great at anything because they have a messed-up view of what it means to be humble or meek. They think you can't be both great and humble at the same time. Your *acting* meek doesn't serve the world; *being* meek does. Meekness lies in knowing your GIFT was given to you by your Father, and that you did nothing to deserve it. Your GIFT is not about you. It is about making a difference.

When I ask people what they want to do, almost all of them reply they don't know. What they do know is that they want to make a difference somehow. They want to know they have something of value they can contribute. They want to know they are valued, and they want to be appreciated. Isn't that how you feel?

The problem is you pretend to be small and still be significant at the same time. If you have something in you that is brilliant, and for which you are recognized as being great, then having a false sense of humility so you won't stick out in a crowd doesn't help anything. Real humility is using your GIFT to its fullest potential, so the maximum number of people can benefit from it. You won't need to seek recognition, because you will naturally be recognized for your GIFT. If you still feel the need to seek recognition, then you are probably not operating in a God-given GIFT.

> **Real humility is using your GIFT to its fullest potential, so the maximum number of people can benefit from it.**

Have you ever held back your talent so that you didn't overshadow someone else? If so, why did you do it? Was it to make the other person feel better? If so, how many people benefited from your holding back? How many more would have been blessed if you had let your light shine instead?

I think all of us can relate to the feeling of holding back to not upset the apple cart at some time or other. The question is why? Sometimes it is because we are not confident in our GIFT. Sometimes we are afraid of offending people if we overshadow them. Sometimes this fear is so great we don't even look for what we do well or seek the GIFT we have been blessed with.

So, what's the point? The point is that our biggest fear is not that we are inadequate. Our biggest fear is that we have something awesome inside us and that it may overwhelm us and take us somewhere we may think we do not want to go. That fear is the biggest reason people stay stuck where they are and have a difficult time overcoming inertia.

Faith overcomes fear. Faith that you have a GIFT, and faith that you have an awesome purpose. When you discover your GIFT, you'll see that any fear you may have will start to fade, and hope starts to take its place. Hope that you really can make a difference. They say that faith comes by hearing, so let me tell you one more time: you have a GIFT and it is perfect for you.

Skills Versus Talent

One of the ways to describe your Special GIFT is that it is the one talent you possess that can be developed to greatness. The word *talent* can mean different things to different people, and some incorrectly use the words *skill*, *ability*, or *aptitude* interchangeably with the word *talent* adding to the confusion. We need to be more specific for the next section to make sense.

Skill

Skill means you have the ability to use your knowledge effectively. Skills are learned. As a Marine, I learned to be a good pilot. I came back from most missions drenched in sweat, and physically and mentally exhausted. Flying was not natural to me; it was hard work. On the same missions I flew, other pilots came back completely exhilarated. I had to work my butt off while they were having fun. That is because they were naturally talented, where I was skilled. My abilities were all learned, while theirs were natural.

The instructors in flight school recognized the dangers of becoming overwhelmed with tasks while flying a military aircraft. They trained us to prioritize our tasks. The most important task was to Aviate, then to Navigate, and then to Communicate. They would often purposely overwhelm us to see if we could prioritize correctly. The more experience we had, the more skilled we became in these areas.

The flight training never stopped. No matter how seasoned a pilot you are in the military there are always new skills to learn and to hone. I went from Aviate, Navigate, Communicate to learning how to fight my aircraft (use its weapons systems effectively), then to do it at night, then to do it off a ship, then to fight a section (two) aircraft, and then a division (four aircraft). I think you get the point. Developing these skills was all hard work for me. For some of my buddies it was just natural.

Most people try to "make it," or survive on learned skills. Relying on skills to survive is a response to the Industrial Age. In the Industrial Age, people were paid to do a specific task, and their income depended on what the task was worth to the company. Keeping your skills updated with technology is becoming more and more difficult. It requires constantly going back for more education to sharpen those skills. If you aren't passionate about the skills your job requires, this can become a real chore.

On the other hand, using your GIFT is natural to you. Rather than having to constantly update skills as a requirement for your career field, when you have a GIFT in that field you will want to constantly learn and find new ways to give your GIFT. You'll also find opportunities coming to you because of your GIFT, rather than you chasing open jobs for which many people are competing.

Ability

Ability is the quality or state of being able. So, if you have the ability to do something, it means you can do it; that it is possible. However, just because you can do something doesn't mean you like doing it. How many times have you heard teachers explain to parents that they don't understand why their children don't get better grades? After all, they have the ability! Or how often do we see athletes who have abilities well beyond their performances? So, you might be able to do something, but ability, by itself, is not a true indicator of success.

Some people don't think they can do anything well. They're wrong; they either haven't found it yet or they don't realize that what they do well has value. Other people say they can do several things well. I believe them, and it can be a real problem. Only one of the things you do well is your GIFT. The other things, while they may be good, are distractions. Being good at a lot of things is one of the biggest reasons people don't find their GIFT.

Aptitude

Aptitude is having the capacity for learning something. If you have the aptitude for something, you have the ability to learn about it, and it makes sense to you. One of the most common tests that school guidance counselors and career placement professionals use is some form of an aptitude test. Sometimes, they call these personality tests, but they are heavily skewed in the direction of available career fields and are not really personality tests.

These tests attempt to measure your aptitude for doing certain kinds of work. You may have an aptitude for mechanical work, but have no desire for that kind of career. You may have an aptitude for learning languages, but a career as an interpreter seems very boring to you. My all-time favorite is this: You may have an aptitude for being an accountant, with a guarantee of always having a job, but the idea of doing accounting work as a career doesn't appeal to you at all.

The military uses an aptitude test for people who want to enlist. It is called the Armed Services Vocational Aptitude Battery (ASVAB). It is one of the most widely used aptitude tests in the world and supposedly measures strengths, weaknesses, and potential for future success. So, what does the military use these tests for? They use the ASVAB test to determine which career field they choose for you. In reality, these tests are a measure of how much you learned in high school and have little to do with your personality or strengths. For example, if you score low in the math and science portion of the ASVAB test, your chances of going into a technical field are low.

Talent

The word *talent* means having skills, abilities, and aptitudes, but it also means something much more. The word *talent* comes from the Greek word *talanton*. A *talanton* was a scale or a balance used for measuring the mass of things. The Greeks and the Romans referred to a talent as a measure of gold or silver; and during the first century AD a talent of silver was equal to 58.9 kilograms (about 130 pounds), worth about fifteen years of wages.

Another way to describe a talent is as a unit of value. While we can say someone's talent may be a skill, ability, or an aptitude, if it cannot be converted it into something of value then it is not a talent. Talent is a natural (not learned) ability that has value.

The most valuable thing you possess is the way you think. Your greatest talent, the only one that can be developed to greatness, is a reflection of the way you think. That talent does not diminish with age. It is your Special GIFT.

You can have an aptitude for a certain kind of work but have no desire to engage in it. You can learn skills in several areas and not want to use them. But your Special GIFT is different. That's a talent you want to develop and you desire to use every chance you get.

Spiritual Money

(No, this isn't about giving to charity or about some religious thing.)

The best book I have read on the subject of finding one's GIFT is Robert Kiyosaki's *Before You Quit Your Job*. I know it may seem an unlikely source, but in the middle of the book, Kiyosaki has a discussion with his "Rich Dad" about the three kinds of money. I encourage you to read the book for yourself, but I will paraphrase the parts that relate to finding your GIFT. Kiyosaki says there are three kinds of money:

Competitive money

Cooperative money

Spiritual money

Competitive money is what most people work for, and it involves competing against others. Competition takes place at the bottom levels of Maslow's Hierarchy of Needs. It is also the kind of money people attain by using skills. Cooperative money involves teamwork and cooperating with others rather than competing. This is a little higher up the Hierarchy of Needs. The third and highest kind of money is what he calls Spiritual money. This is money created in response to a higher calling; work that God wants to be done. Your purpose.

While he calls it spiritual money, it isn't about money at all. Kiyosaki says, *"It's about doing a job, not because you want to do it, but because it must be done, and you know down deep in your soul that you're the one who is supposed to do it."* Kiyosaki goes on to say, *"if you were truly committed to solving the problem, the invisible forces of the universe, of God, might come to your support. Magic might happen in your life.*

"People you never met before come to join forces with you—not for the money, but for the mission. One of the keys to attracting the invisible spiritual forces is to be dedicated to giving your GIFT. Your GIFT is a special God-given talent. Something you are the best at. A talent God gave especially to you."

What Is Your Special GIFT?

This is the perfect place to properly define **GIFT**. Your GIFT is a natural talent you possess. You may have several natural talents, which can be a good thing, but being good at several things often confuses people who are seeking their GIFT because they can do several things well. Your Special GIFT is the one talent that:

Stands out above the rest.

You might be good at several things, but you do one of them without effort and with the greatest results.

Can be developed to greatness.

The more you develop your GIFT the better it gets. Making it a hobby, spending most of your free time related to it, makes your GIFT more and more valuable.

You find fulfilling.

When you use your GIFT, it makes you feel good, and you enjoy it. It doesn't feel like work. "Where your treasure (GIFT) is, there will your heart be also."

You would be willing to dedicate your life to.

You might retire from a job, but no one retires from a GIFT. Using it is a lifelong passion.

Is the result of your unique way of thinking.

It is not just what you do, but how you do it, why you do it, the passion with which you do it, and it is determined by the unique way you think.

Now the BIG question: How do you find this God-given talent, your GIFT? Aren't you wondering that? You already have the first piece of the answer; your personality. Remember, your personality is another God-given gift. He predisposed you to behave in a certain way, on purpose.

The next step is to discover the particular talent at which you are the best; the one you are supposed to develop to greatness. Tom Rath, the author of *StrengthsFinder 2.0*, calls the talents that you do best your "Strengths." The findings in his book are the result of the Gallup organization's forty-year study of human strengths, in which they surveyed more than ten million people worldwide and identified thirty-four different strengths that someone could possess.

Gallup® has an online strengths assessment tool called Clifton-Strengths. The assessment will accurately identify and order your thirty-four talents from greatest to lowest. The chances that someone else has the same top five talents as you, and in the same order, is one in thirty-three million. According to Gallup, the odds that someone has all thirty-four of your talents in the same order is 1 in 259 septillion (259 x 10^{36}) or 259,000,000,000,000,000,000,000,000,000,000,000,0 00!

What Rath calls your top talent, I call your GIFT. When your GIFT is backed by your other talents I think you can see just how unique you are. This assessment tool is invaluable, I highly recommend it, and **it is central to discovering your Special GIFT**.

Most people are either unaware of their talents or are unable to describe them. How important do you think it would be to find out the top God-given talent you possess—your GIFT?

Far too many people go an entire lifetime with their GIFT still undiscovered. There is a short story from Mark Twain that describes why finding your GIFT is so important to making a difference. It goes like this:

> *A man died and met Saint Peter at the Pearly Gates.*
>
> *He said, "Saint Peter, I have been interested in military history for many years. Who was the greatest general of all time?"*
>
> *Saint Peter quickly responded, "Oh that's a simple question. It's that man right over there."*
>
> *"You must be mistaken," responded the man, now very perplexed. "I knew that man on earth, and he was just a common laborer."*
>
> *"That's right, my friend," assured Saint Peter. "He would have been the greatest general of all time if he had been a general."*

When I took the CliftonStrengths assessment, I was surprised at how accurate it was. What you will find is that your GIFT (that top talent) lines up perfectly with your personality. Without the right personality, your GIFT could not be used effectively. That's because your personality is a function of behavior, while your GIFT describes your unique way of thinking.

> # Your personality is a function of behavior, while your GIFT describes your unique way of thinking.

You will be amazed at how much your GIFT (the top talent in the profile you receive from the CliftonStrengths assessment) is a natural part of who you are. However, we often take our talents for granted and compare our weaknesses to another's GIFT. The very people you envy look at your GIFT and marvel. Wait until you develop your GIFT and start using it with purpose. You will see what I mean.

I always understand concepts better when someone can show me an example. Using myself as an example:

TJ's CliftonStrengths talents are

> Maximizer
>
> Individualization
>
> Ideation
>
> Futuristic
>
> Relator

The top talent in my assessment is Maximizer. A Maximizer thinks differently from the thirty-three other talents listed in the assessment. This is the description of a Maximizer from my assessment:

"People who are especially talented in the Maximizer theme focus on strengths as a way to stimulate personal and group excellence. They seek to transform something strong into something superb. You likely notice the unique traits that differentiate one person from everyone else.

You have little patience with people who stereotype others into general categories. You prefer to describe individuals with specific and vivid details. You deal with each individual on a personal level. You instinctively know what someone is feeling, based on the person's words, deeds, or body gestures."

The assessment also provides **Ideas for Action** for each of your top five talents. Here are a few of the ideas for action of a Maximizer:

- *Problem-solving might drain your energy and enthusiasm.*

- *Study success. Deliberately spend time with people who have discovered their strengths.*

- *Don't find what is broken and fix it. Keep your focus on long-term relationships and goals.*

Many make a career out of picking the low-hanging fruit of short-term success, but your Maximizer talents will be most energized and effective as you turn top potential into true and lasting greatness.

- *Seek roles in which you are helping people succeed.*

You will find that some of the ideas for action leap off the page at you, either because you already do them or because you don't, but know you should. Other ideas don't do anything for you right now. Pay close attention to the ones that stick out and try to put them into action as soon as you can. Also, don't just pay attention to the ideas for your top strength; study the ideas for the other four talents as well. I'll bet you find some gems in there.

You will also find that your GIFT not only fits perfectly with your personality, but it helps to explain aspects of who you are that you may not have considered. It can show you how to benefit more from the real you. Take a look at the following chart.

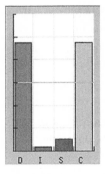

The left side is a representation of my personality profile. A "**C-D**" personality is a natural problem solver. My personality assessment says a "**C-D**" personality has the *"ability to identify potential problems and detect errors. He can bring logic and understanding while providing logical steps to evaluate and analyze information. He excels at developing a strategy and methods to solve problems."*

Personality and GIFT

Personality – Creative Pattern

- **Emotions:** accepts aggression, restrains expression
- **Goal:** dominance, unique accomplishments
- **Influences others by:** ability to develop systems and create innovative approaches
- **Value to organization:** <u>Problem solving</u> ability initiates or designs changes
- **Overuses:** bluntness, critical or condescending attitude
- **Under Pressure:** becomes bored with routine work, sulks when restrained, acts independently
- **Fears:** lack of influence, failure to achieve their standards

Your desire for tangible results is counterbalanced by equally strong <u>drive for perfection</u>. Foresight when focusing on projects brings about change. You demonstrate <u>considerable planning ability</u>. You may not be concerned about social poise, and <u>may be cool, aloof and blunt</u>

GIFT – Maximizer Ideas for action

- Problem solving might drain your energy and enthusiasm
- Don't find what is broken and fix it. Keep your focus on long-term relationships and goals
- Many make a career out of picking the low-hanging fruit of short-term success, but your Maximizer talents will be most energized and effective as you turn top potential into true and lasting greatness
- Seek roles in which you are helping people succeed

The DISC assessment I took calls my **C-D** personality a "Creative Pattern." How have the people I have worked for interpreted that? I'm the guy employers would send in to find out what was wrong and fix it. When I chose the wrong career in sales, guess what I did? I tried to fix sales approaches or strategies, find, or develop better products and solve problems my customers were having. Since many businesses are very short-term focused, rarely looking beyond the next couple of months, my bosses wanted me to put my efforts toward immediate returns. They realized I could help them find problems, but they wanted short-term solutions with immediate results.

My CliftonStrengths profile paints a different picture. It acknowledges that I have problem-solving abilities, but it says I would not be using my GIFT if I chase short-term results. It also says to focus on long-term relationships instead of trying to fix what is broken. I should look for what is good and try to make it superb. Instead of focusing on sales, I should look for ways to help people.

Do you see that you can be operating in your personality, at least to some degree, and yet not be using your GIFT? When that happens, you'll find your work exhausting. However, when you use your GIFT in your work you will find it exhilarating and fulfilling.

As with the personality profiles discussed earlier, your GIFT is identified by your most dominant trait, but the other four talents help to support it. Using my CliftonStrengths assessment as an example, the top "talent" (GIFT) and the other four supporting talents are:

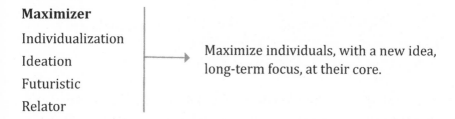

Maximizer

Individualization

Ideation

Futuristic

Relator

Maximize individuals, with a new idea, long-term focus, at their core.

I've already described a Maximizer talent, here is a brief description of the other four talents:

Individualization—intrigued by the unique qualities of each person.

Ideation—fascinated by ideas and finding the simple concepts beneath the complex.

Futuristic—loves to peer over the horizon; "wouldn't it be great if...?"

Relator—wants to understand their feelings, goals, fears, and dreams.

Your combination of top five talents describes your unique GIFT. In this case, Maximizer is affected by the other four talents of Individualization, Ideation, Futuristic and Relator. This combination of "talents" makes for a person GIFTed as a Maximizer who sees people as individuals with their unique potentials, who also has the ability to come up with unique ideas and creativity to use his GIFT, thinks long term and can see where things are going, and relates well to people on their level.

Can you see how those four talents can combine with Maximizer to form a unique GIFT? What if the supporting four talents were:

Maximizer

Competitive

Command

Disciple

Focus

Chances are that a person with this GIFT profile would have a very high **D** personality, and their Maximizer GIFT would be used to drive something forward with a focused, disciplined competitive force.

Even though both of these people would have a Maximizer GIFT, how they would employ that GIFT would be radically different. Their purposes would be different as would how they make a difference.

How Your GIFT Fits on a Team

CliftonStrengths has identified thirty-four different talents. They have discovered that the talents could further be divided into four main groups. The talents within each domain group he calls *Themes* and are related to each other to some degree. The chart below shows the different domain groups and themes.

Your GIFT is meant to work in harmony with people who have other GIFTs. That way no one must be all things to all people. Ideally, you should work with people who have talents that you don't have. That allows you to continue to develop your GIFT and not be stuck in the unproductive pursuit of improving your weaknesses.

You will find that the best teams have people with talents in all of the four major domain groups. This is true whether the team is at work, in an organization, at church, or in a marriage. In the chart below, I have highlighted my talents in black and underlined them. My wife's talents are highlighted in black, but not underlined.

4 Domain Groups
34 Themes
TJ / Mary

Executing	Influencing	Relationship	Strategic
Achiever	**Activator**	Adaptability	Analytical
Arranger	Command	Developer	Context
Belief	Communicative	Connectedness	**Futuristic**
Consistency	Competitive	Empathy	**Ideation**
Deliberative	**Maximizer**	Harmony	Input
Discipline	Self-assurance	Includer	Intellection
Focus	Significance	**Individualization**	Learner
Responsibility	Woo	Positivity	Strategic
Restorative		**Relator**	
		Relator	

Notice that I have talents in the Influencing, Relationship, and Strategic domain groups but none in the Executing group. As I use my GIFT, I know to actively look for people who are naturally strong in one or more of the talents listed in the Executing domain group to be more successful. My wife, on the other hand, has talents in all the groups except Strategic. Fortunately, we have all the domain groups covered to some degree between the two of us and duplicate the theme of Relator.

Consequently, we work well together as both business partners and a married couple.

As you employ your GIFT, it is good to keep this chart in mind and to remember that no man is an island. Paraphrasing Saint Paul, *we are all individual members of the body, but God has placed us in the body as He desires so that individuals, working together, can cause the whole body to grow.* This means that your GIFT is needed, not just for your benefit, but for others as well. When you develop your GIFT to its full potential, you become a part of something greater than yourself that makes a difference.

Every person whom the world views as great had one thing in common: They were focused on what they did exceptionally well. Ralph Waldo Emerson called it **finding your best self**. Napoleon Hill called it a **definite major purpose**. Saint Paul called it **the one thing I do**. Regardless of what you choose to call it, your Special GIFT unlocks the door to your abundant life. BUT, to receive the greatest benefit of your GIFT it has to be used in combination with the GIFTs of others.

You Are Chosen

An interesting aspect of finding your Special GIFT is that you were chosen for it. You do not choose your GIFT; it was chosen for you and given to you from your birth. This way of thinking can rub us Americans the wrong way, so let me explain.

> You do not choose your GIFT; it was chosen for you and given to you from your birth.

If you were raised in the United States, you might have been brought up to believe in self-determination and that you are the captain of your fate. To some degree, that is true. You do have the ability to choose, and you can say "no" to things you don't want to do. Our Declaration of Independence states that we have been endowed by our Creator with certain unalienable Rights, that among these are Life, Liberty, and the pursuit of Happiness. As a republic, we have more liberty to choose our destinies than most countries.

Even so, to say you can do anything that you put your mind to is not entirely correct. As it says in *StrengthsFinder 2.0*, "A revision to the you-can-be-anything-you-want-to-be maxim might be more accurate: *You **cannot** be anything you want to be—but you **can** be more of who you already are.*"

"You **cannot** be anything you want to be — but you **can** be more of who you already are."
Tom Rath

You must work within the talents and attributes you possess. If you are five feet tall, have no vertical jump, and you can't shoot, your chances of being an NBA superstar are remote, no matter how much you want it. Your physical size, your personality, and your talent are gifts you were born with. Your choice involves using them and developing them. You cannot choose to be six feet tall if your mature height is five feet. Likewise, you cannot be a great singer if you were born tone-deaf. In the United States, you have the liberty to pursue things, even if you have no gifts in those areas—but that does not mean you will be successful.

My point is this: you are who you are, and you have a very special GIFT for a reason. The sooner you accept your GIFT, and who you really are, rather than wishing for talents and attributes that are not yours, the sooner you will discover your purpose. The sooner you develop your GIFT, that one talent you do best, the sooner you will fulfill your purpose and receive the prize that was set aside just for you. Don't be like the man in Mark Twain's story, accepting life as a common laborer when he was born to be the greatest general.

The Work

Anyone who is recognized as being truly GIFTed has had to go through the hard work to develop that GIFT. Whether the GIFTed person is an athlete, a musician, a motivational speaker, a writer, an attorney, or a salesman, they have had to perfect their craft to become great. Even though it is hard work, the one who develops their GIFT does it as a labor of love.

> Even though it is hard work, the one who develops their GIFT does it as a labor of love.

A person with a GIFT is the one still practicing when the rest of the team has gone home. She is the one doing scales and vocal training when no one is listening, and he is the one making extra sales calls when no one else would dream of it. GIFTed people put in the extra effort, not because they have to, but because they want to. They love what they do and they want to be the best.

My mother was a competitive amateur figure skater in Germany and turned professional at twenty-four years old. She told me stories of practicing ice skating in meat lockers as a little girl because there was no other ice to skate on in post-World War II East Germany. When I was in high school, Mom became an figure-skating coach in Northern Virginia. I remember her leaving the house at four in the morning to help her figure skating students prepare for their next skating test.

While I thought she was nuts, she thought it was all part of what it took to be a great skater. She loved it, and her skaters loved her.

Have you ever known a musician? Have you noticed he or she is always doing something with or about music? It could be practicing, checking out someone else's technique, or talking with other musicians, but a good musician is always engaged in music. The musician speaks a whole different language, and even their thoughts are musical.

How about computer geeks? Not everyone can be a great athlete or musician, but most of us have run into someone who just thinks like a computer. Such people intuitively understand how networks work, how code is written, and how to solve huge business problems by using computers and developing software. To me, computers are a necessary part of today's life, but they are usually more infuriating than a source of enjoyment. To a computer geek (they call themselves geeks, so I mean no disrespect in using that term), studying computer hardware and software is their passion. A computer geek never seems to talk about anything else.

I worked with a young lady who was GIFTed at tracking data. She could use every facet of what Microsoft had developed to track even the smallest of details. Her presentation of data wasn't just on spreadsheets, but on bar graphs, colored pie charts, and any other way the data could be presented so it would make sense. She did her work at the office, at home, on vacation...it didn't seem to matter to her. The thought of me having to do it was a nightmare, but she loved it. I certainly appreciated her phenomenal work.

The work required to develop your GIFT may look like a herculean effort to someone else, but to you, it is part of what you do. You enjoy the hard work because the reward for using your GIFT makes it all worthwhile. Sometimes the reward is just the knowledge that there is no one as good as you are in your field. As King Solomon said, "A man's gift makes room for him and brings him before great men."

Last Thoughts on GIFT

I have a couple of last thoughts for you regarding your GIFT. You were created with your personality, your GIFT, and a desire as part of your original design. They were given to you for you to reach your full potential. However, you can choose to use them or you can choose to do things your way (which usually means the way someone else convinced you was better). The great thing is that your personality, GIFT, and desire will always be inside you, even if you choose not to use them.

As a little kid, my father loved me even when I was too young to love him back, and even when I messed up. That's called unconditional love. Likewise, your Father will love you even if you choose not to use what He has given you. He won't take back the GIFT He gave you. It's yours to use to get the prize of what you want, even if you don't know what that is yet.

People are struggling because they don't know what they already have inside them. I don't want that to be you.

Chapter 7
Purpose

Purpose is defined as the reason that something exists. That's pretty straightforward. My definition of your purpose is also simple but includes how you can find it. Your purpose is to employ your special and unique GIFT.

> Your purpose is to employ your Special GIFT. It is "**what**" you were born to do.

Discovering your purpose involves more than just knowing your GIFT. Knowing it is great, but if you want to find your purpose you will have to use the GIFT you have been given. As you do you'll begin to realize that you didn't acquire your GIFT by something you did—you were born with it. Yes, you made an effort to develop it, but you developed what was already there. That is called being a good steward.

Your purpose is "what" you were born to do. It is the reason you were created. But we need to be more specific.

I recently asked an acquaintance in my hometown if he knew his purpose. He is about twenty-five years old, has a job, and is also going to college for an associate's degree. Without hesitation, he said he knew his purpose. To tell the truth I was a little shocked; I didn't expect him to give me an answer. When I asked him to tell me what he thought his purpose was, he said, "My purpose is to help people."

Okay, nice try, but dumb answer (I didn't tell him that). I politely asked him how he was going to help people. Silence followed until his friend chimed in. His friend said he was going to help people with his smile. My acquaintance did have a great smile, but I don't think either he or his friend had given the subject much thought.

Purpose Takes Away Excuses

The best book on purpose I have read is by Myles Monroe. In Monroe's book *In Pursuit of Purpose*, he makes an amazing and somewhat controversial statement:

> *"Your natural inclinations to socialize with people or to seek solitude, to think with your mind or to do things with your hands, to communicate with words or to express yourself through various art forms, to come up with the ideas or to put them into action, to lead or to follow, to inspire or to manage, to calculate or to demonstrate are part of your makeup and your personality from the time God chose to make you and designed you in a particular way. They relate to your purpose, which is a natural, innate, intimate part of who you are. You are designed for your purpose. You are perfect for your purpose.*

> *"Your purpose, your abilities and your outlook on life cannot be separated, because your purpose determines how you will function, which establishes how you are designed, which is related to your potential, which is connected to your natural abilities.... Everything you naturally have and inherently are is necessary for you to fulfill your purpose. Your height, race, skin color, language, physical features, and intellectual capacity are all designed for your purpose."*

It is amazing to realize you were created with the personality and abilities to live a life of purpose, and that your natural attributes (race, skin color, language, etc.) are perfect for you, and actually necessary for you to fulfill your purpose. This can be considered controversial because it takes away a lot of excuses. Once you know your Special GIFT and start to employ it there is no reason to remain trapped in the basic needs of Maslow's Hierarchy of Needs.

> ## "You are perfectly designed for your purpose."
> ### Myles Monroe

Purpose Isn't Taught

One would think something as important as finding your GIFT and employing it for a purpose would be taught somewhere, but it isn't. I have seen plenty of people and organizations that talk about purpose—what it is, and how important it is, etc.—but no one could show me how to find mine.

The fact that the subject is a mystery, without answers or a process, may be a contributing factor to the general lack of awareness of the concept that everyone has a Special GIFT. If the only thing that people can do is tell you what purpose is, but not how to find it or develop it, then it's no wonder that one's Special GIFT isn't something we talk about every day.

I want to change all that. Joe Purpose was created to help you become aware that we are all supposed to live a life of purpose. Joe (your) Purpose is exciting, fun, and fulfilling. He is uplifting and positive, as is your purpose. Your purpose is the key to your joy and your success.

The will to find and live with purpose comes from the knowledge that you have a Special GIFT. The Joe Purpose character is a symbol of that idea.

Why Pursue Your Purpose?

Some estimates are that only 2% of the population knows their purpose and are pursuing it. What makes the 2% different from the 98%? Why do some assume the responsibility to find what they desire in life and others don't? Can those numbers change?

There is a small percentage of the population that seems to pop out of their mother's womb knowing exactly what they were born to do with their lives. They make the rest of us look bad. If you were to ask them how they know, they wouldn't be able to tell you; they assume everybody knows. They wonder what is wrong with someone who doesn't know exactly what they desire. They can't conceive of living without passion in pursuing a purpose. Having a discussion with these people will just end up making both of you frustrated—I know, because I've tried.

There is an even smaller number of people who have tripped over their purpose accidentally. How did they find their purpose, and how can you find yours? There is not a one-size-fits-all answer.

"Purpose is the destination that prompts the journey."

Myles Monroe

A Life with Purpose

Why do you need to know your purpose? It seems that the majority of people don't realize their purpose and still manage to get through life, so why do you even need to find your purpose? Everyone says that life is a struggle, so what difference does having a purpose make?

It is often people without a purpose that you hear talking about how hard life can be and all about their struggles. You rarely hear a person that knows their purpose speak about struggle. You have a choice—you can either struggle through life, and at the end wonder what the trip was for, or you can live with purpose.

10 Reasons Why You Should Live with Purpose

1. **Your income is directly related to the time spent developing and pursuing your purpose.**

   What is the difference between the income of an average skilled person and the top person in that profession? It is usually an order of magnitude. For example, an average skilled baseball player will never make it to the major leagues. Of those who make it to Major League Baseball, an average professional player (obviously very skilled) typically gets one hit in every four times at bat for a batting average of .250. His income can be between $3 million and $4 million a year. However, a GIFTed Major League player hits over .300 with a salary of $28 million a year. The difference is only one extra hit every twenty times at bat, and normally the result of developing their GIFT.

   The same distinction occurs in almost every profession. Those who are not using their GIFT may be skilled at what they do, may earn a reasonable salary, and may even like what they do. However, those that are using their GIFT are usually at the top of their pay scale and love what they do.

2. **With purpose, you will make a difference.**

   When I ask people what they want to do, almost no one knows. However, what they all seem to agree on is that they want to make a difference. Making a difference requires belonging to or affecting something bigger than yourself. It means being a part of a vision that matters to you. It also means knowing that you contribute to that vision in some significant way. The meaningful way that you contribute is your purpose. If you don't find your purpose, then your desire to make a difference will not be fulfilled.

3. With purpose, you will have more control.

When you don't know your purpose in life you'll find yourself either just going with the flow (drifting) or allowing others to make decisions about your life for you. Sometimes the ones you allow to make decisions for you will manipulate you for their gain. However, when you know what you want and where you are going you can chart your course. It becomes much more difficult for anyone to manipulate you. When you know your purpose, you make choices that align with that purpose, and you make progress towards your destiny.

4. With purpose, you will have more focus.

One of the biggest things you'll find when you begin to operate in your purpose is that decision making becomes easier. That's because you'll start to evaluate everything based on whether it coincides with where you want to go. You will naturally be less inclined to waste time, money, and energy on things outside your purpose. This is called focus. One of the side benefits of focus is that it can give you more time because you'll find you waste less of it on distractions.

5. With purpose, you will be more content.

Being content means being satisfied with what you have. When you know your purpose, you will become confident that it will provide the things you need. As already stated, it will increase your income, but more than that is the satisfaction that comes from doing what you were born to do and its benefits to others.

6. With purpose, you will be more peaceful.

Peace is an internal condition, one that comes from being satisfied with yourself. Not being overly concerned with affairs that are outside of your purpose will considerably reduce the amount of stress on your life, while knowing you are on track to do what you are called to do creates excitement. Regardless of the challenges around you, knowing your purpose allows you to weather any storm and stay on course.

7. With purpose, you will be more confident.

When you know who you are and why you are on the planet, you will exude confidence. You will see that you aren't an expert at everything, and don't have to be. When it comes to your particular GIFT, you are the expert, having devoted time and energy into developing your GIFT that others have not. You become so sure of yourself that no one can rock your boat. Since you know it is a GIFT, you'll also have the humility that many will find attractive. A side benefit of this kind of confidence is that it will draw people to you. This will become a valuable asset in accomplishing your purpose, as no one can do anything significant by themselves.

8. With purpose, you will have better relationships.

Since a prerequisite to finding your purpose is to know who you are, that, combined with the confidence you'll exude from understanding your purpose, will be very attractive. The relationships you form, whether personal or professional, will be based on the real you without ulterior motives. You will find that when you are genuine with other people they usually reciprocate. This makes for relationships based on the truth. When you are sincere with other people, those that are not in agreement with your purpose will tell you. Knowing where you stand with other people makes finding the right partners much easier.

9. With purpose, you will be able to have unity.

Unity is a necessary ingredient in a marriage, a business, a government, and a church. When you know your purpose, you will find your thoughts elevated by others who are in harmony with that purpose. Your purpose and corresponding GIFT will need the GIFTs of others to work together to make a vision or cause a reality. When each person in a marriage, a leadership team, or a church knows their purpose, you will find that jealousy and competition cease, and cooperation takes over. The vision is what becomes important, and each person's purpose is a relevant part of that vision becoming a reality.

10. With purpose, you will have more faith.

You may have heard the saying that "faith without works is dead." Well, here is why. Faith can be defined as having complete trust or belief in someone or something. Purpose is defined as employing your GIFT in a vision or cause. When you know that you have a GIFT and that you are supposed to employ that GIFT, then the faith to do so comes with the GIFT. People end up focusing on having faith when they really should be focused on the GIFT and who gave it to them.

The faith to employ your GIFT comes with the GIFT.

If you knew you had a God-given GIFT, then there would be no question that you would be expected to use it. If God gave it to you, wouldn't you have great confidence that whatever He wanted it applied to would be successful? How much faith would you have in the outcome? So then, the faith to move mountains comes from the knowledge that you have the GIFT and authority to do so.

A Life Without Purpose

Those are some of the reasons that we need to know our purpose, but what happens when we live without purpose? Here are 10 results of living without purpose:

1. Drifting

According to James Allen, author of *As a Man Thinketh*,

"Until thought is linked with purpose there is no intelligent accomplishment. With the majority, the bark of thought is allowed to 'drift' upon the ocean of life. Aimlessness is a vice, and such drifting must not continue for him who would steer clear of catastrophe and destruction.

"They who have no central purpose in their life fall an easy prey to petty worries, fears, troubles, and self-pitying's, all of which are indications of weakness, which lead, just as surely as deliberately planned sins (though by a different route), to failure, unhappiness, and loss, for weakness cannot persist in a power-evolving universe."

When you live without purpose, the only things to live for are survival and pleasure, and neither lasts.

2. Procrastination/indecision

If you are not living with purpose you will probably delay and obsess over major decisions. Sometimes it is because you can't make up your mind and sometimes it is because you don't want to deal with it. People who have a purpose make decisions quickly because they are on a mission. Delaying a decision by procrastinating could delay them from achieving their goals.

Sometimes people will be indecisive because they aren't used to thinking for themselves. They need to get the advice and approval of others before they make a decision. The opinions of others do not sway people who live with purpose, so they are usually more decisive.

3. Lack of commitment

Not being able to commit to a relationship or a job comes from waiting for something better to arrive down the road. Why commit to something or someone when there's a chance something better could come your way? A better-looking spouse, a better-paying job, someone who understands you better. Waiting for something better is the same thing as drifting. It is the result of not having a purpose, so you don't move in a direction with determination; you just let things happen. You don't expect anything so you take whatever comes your way.

However, when you know who you are, what you want, and where you are going, then your commitment is to your purpose. Your purpose will drive your choices of jobs and relationships. You will choose a job that can help you to develop and possibly allow you to use your GIFT. You will choose relationships with people who support your dreams and desires, not just people who look good.

Until you know your purpose, and the purpose of the one you want to marry, you're probably better off waiting. The awesome part about knowing your purpose is discovering who will be attracted to you specifically because of your purpose. That kind of attraction is worth committing to.

4. Lack of excellence

Even if you are one of those people who says they give 100% on a task, you won't know what your full potential is until you know your GIFT and your purpose. Since most people don't know their purpose, they think that doing enough to get by is good enough. To them, that is 100%. They might work hard at their job, but after 5 p.m. work is over, and now they are on their time.

The person who loves what they do is probably using their GIFT. They get enjoyment and fulfillment from their work, so putting in a little more time and going the extra mile is not labor for them. It's what they do. Just "good enough" is never good enough; their goal is excellence.

5. Fear

If you are afraid of losing your job, losing your spouse, wondering where you are at in your relationship, or worry about money, then you probably have not found your purpose. Anyone who lives with purpose has confidence that others don't understand. That's because they know where they are going and they know they have what it takes to get there.

> ## Anyone who lives with purpose has confidence that others don't understand.

That's not to say that these people don't have setbacks and failures, but when they do it is just an inconvenience on the road to fulfilling their purpose. The things that crush most people don't stop a person with purpose. That's because they have the ability to endure. That ability is called passion, something everyone with purpose possesses.

6. Faithlessness

When you see someone who has no faith in themselves, no faith in others, and no faith in God, it is a sure sign they don't know their purpose.

When something is created or is manufactured, it usually comes with instructions. The instructions tell you who made the product, what it does, and how to use it. If you don't read the instruction manual for a complicated product, there is a pretty good chance you won't use it properly. That means that a perfectly good product may never fulfill its purpose.

People are very complicated creations that also come with an instruction manual. Most people don't bother to read the instructions so they don't know who made them, what they were created to do, or how they fit in. If they don't know those things about themselves then they won't know those things about other people either, or even care.

On the other hand, when you know your purpose you will realize that others also have a purpose. You will know that your Creator gave you a GIFT and a purpose for its use. If you follow the instructions you can be very confident in using your GIFT and the success it will create. That kind of confidence is called faith.

7. Poor health

I had the privilege of having dinner with Dr. Don Colbert, MD, and his wife one evening in Chicago. Besides being board-certified in family practice and anti-aging medicine, Don is a *New York Times* bestselling author. In his book *Stress Less*, he says that between 75% and 90% of all visits to primary care physicians are related to stress disorders.

> ## "Between 75% and 90% of all visits to primary care physicians are related to stress disorders."
> ### Dr. Don Colbert

Everything from depression, anxiety, eating disorders, obesity, type 2 diabetes, heart disease, hypertension, sexual dysfunction, sleep disorders, osteoporosis, alcoholism, PMS, and headaches have stress as one of their root causes.

What we talked about that night at dinner was the effect that not having a purpose has on stress. Observe anyone you know with a purpose, and even though they might be a whirlwind of activity, they won't be stressed. The bottom line is that living with purpose will have a positive effect on your health.

8. Depression

One of the surest signs that so few people know their purpose is the epidemic of depression in our population. According to the Anxiety and Depression Association of America, depression affects more than fifteen million American adults, or about 6.7 percent of the US population age eighteen and older. (Can you believe there is such an organization? Now that's depressing.)

> ## "Purpose creates meaning."
> ### Psychology Today

According to a *Psychology Today* article from July 2016, "purpose creates meaning. And the rhythm that comes with purpose sets into motion physical, emotional and spiritual awakenings that significantly aid well-being."

I've never met a person who knew their purpose who was depressed. They are too busy using and giving their GIFT to be depressed. They are excited about what they have to offer and what they have been called to do.

9. Suicide

First, some horrible facts about suicide. Suicide is the tenth leading cause of death in America. Each year 44,192 Americans die by suicide, and for each death twenty-five more attempt suicide. It costs the US $44 billion annually—not that it can be measured in dollars. Approximately 58,000 Americans were killed in action in Vietnam, but the toll in suicides of the men and women who came home from that conflict is more than 100,000. (We don't know all the facts from the wars in Iraq and Afghanistan yet.) According to suicide.org, untreated depression is the number one cause of suicide.

I have heard experts on this subject speak before large audiences of police officers, who also share unusually high suicide rates. These experts' only solution to the devastating problem is what they call *awareness*. Their solution is that if someone is aware that a person is having suicidal thoughts, then he or she can intervene to stop the suicidal act. While that's all well and good, does it solve the problem?

As with depression, I would challenge anyone to find a person who knew their GIFT, their purpose, and their value to the world that would contemplate suicide. If anything, they would look for more time on the planet, not less.

10. Retirement

Most people today will work careers for forty-five years or longer, in jobs they barely tolerate, in hopes of someday retiring. I realize that is not true of everyone, but many people would rather be somewhere else than at work from eight to five, five days a week, fifty weeks a year.

The retirement they imagine ranges from living the life of the rich and famous to just waking up whenever they want with no one telling them what to do. The unfortunate fact is that retirement for most folks devolves into hoping they die before their money runs out. Retirement for them is a daily battle of worry and fear, and many "wealth coaches" and "investment advisers" and the like prey on that fear.

I am not saying you shouldn't have a wealth coach or an investment adviser, but if you are relying on your taxes to go down because you **have less income** after you retire, there is something wrong with that picture. In case you missed it, the something wrong was having less income.

People who have a purpose do not retire. They continue to give their GIFT even after they leave the employment of a company. Giving one's GIFT always has value, so thinking about your income in your Golden Years should be just that... Golden Years. If you are retired or thinking about it, I would encourage you to read *The New Retirementality* by Mitch Anthony. Once you have found your GIFT, this might change your mind about retiring.

Giving one's GIFT always has value.

So, what's the point?

The point is that finding your purpose has a whole host of benefits. Maybe being aware of these benefits is enough of a catalyst to get you started on the path to finding your purpose. Everybody deserves to find theirs because that is when life really begins.

Chapter 8
Desire and Passion

We often use words in our everyday language without really knowing what they mean. Misusing or not understanding a word can create confusion. For example, if I mention the word *desire*, what is the first thing that comes to mind? Some of you immediately think of something or someone you want. For others, desire is translated as lust.

I'm not sure where I got this, but desire always meant something bad to me. It might be from my early Catholic upbringing and some false image of desires leading me straight to Hell. Napoleon Hill's description of desire is that it should be obsessional and should be developed into a "Burning Desire." That didn't really help the matter since burning and Hell went together.

Definitions

So, to make sure we are all on the same page on the subject of desire, I'm going to use some definitions.

The dictionary defines the word **desire** as **to long for** or **hope** for something. What do "long for" and "hope" mean? The definition of *to long for* or *longing* is a strong, persistent desire or craving, especially for something unattainable or distant. Hope is defined as a feeling of **expectation** and desire for a certain thing to happen.

Passion is closely associated with desire, but what does that mean? I found it interesting that the first definition of *passion*, often capitalized, is the **sufferings** of Christ between the night of the Last Supper and his death. It is also defined as an ardent affection, a strong liking or desire for, or devotion to some activity, object, or concept, or a sexual desire.

Suffering and *passion* did not seem to go together to me, so I had to look up the word *suffer*. (See how confusing this can be?) I thought it meant intense pain, like from torture or a disease. What it really means is to submit to, or to be forced to endure something. It also means to put up with something inevitable or unavoidable.

Taking all of this into account, here is what I mean when I use the words Desire and Passion:

Desire:
a strong, persistent hope and expectation for something.

Knowing who you are and knowing your GIFT activates your hope because you know it is possible. You may not expect to get what you wish or dream for, but you do expect to get what you desire.

Passion:
a strong, active, intense, emotional desire that enables you to endure hardship, even suffering.

Passion gives you the endurance to stay the course and overcome the obstacles that will get in the way of you obtaining the desire of your heart.

There is a proverb that says, "Hope deferred makes the heart grow sick but desire fulfilled is a tree of life." A lot of people have sick hearts these days. They have heart disease, have high blood pressure, take antidepressant medication by the buckets full, and many are suicidal. Even those who aren't depressed are often angry or fearful. There doesn't seem to be a lot of joy in the world.

The same proverb that speaks about sick hearts also has the solution. It says that desire fulfilled is a tree of life. That means that fulfilling your desire brings a long, happy, joyful, and abundant life. So, what do you want? A sick heart or a tree of life? Your choice has to do with your desire.

Desire Is the Starting Point

In his famous book *Think and Grow Rich*, Napoleon Hill says, *"Desire is the starting point of all achievement."* He adds, *"No one is ready for a thing until he believes he can acquire it."* You can't expect lasting success, joy, and fulfillment without desiring and expecting to receive something. To a large degree, even your health depends on your desires.

The main reason that so many people have sick hearts is that they don't expect to get what they desire; they don't have hope. And the reason they don't have hope is that they don't know their identity. Your identity is who you really are, plus your GIFT.

Identity = Who you really are + your GIFT.

When you know who you are and you know your GIFT, you will naturally want to use your GIFT. Wanting to use your GIFT is the desire of your heart. That desire has been inside you for as long as you have had a GIFT—which means from birth. The problem is that most people don't know who they are or their GIFT.

> ## Wanting to use your GIFT is the desire of your heart.

So, if desire is the starting point—or to use an analogy, the first floor of your building—then your identity is the foundation. Without a strong foundation, the building will eventually collapse, but with a sure foundation, a tall and strong structure can be erected.

I think many people take the foundation for granted, as if they already knew their desire. That is not true for most people, so most of us have to take the time to build a strong foundation. That means you need to have a catalyst, discover who you are, and discover your GIFT before you will know your desire.

I love to talk to people about their purpose, but it isn't any easy topic to broach. I've never heard anyone start a conversation about purpose on their own—it just doesn't happen, at least not for me. The way I introduce the idea of purpose to people is to ask them what they do. Most people don't think that is too threatening a question. I then follow up with, "What do you really want to do?"

Since at least 70% of employees are not engaged while at work according to the Gallup organization, I know that most of the people I ask will tell me they are not doing what they really want. If someone asked you what you really want, how would you answer? Most of the time what people will say is that they don't know, but they wish they could figure it out. It's not an easy question to answer.

Rather than guess, I wanted to know what people really want. Frank Luntz, famous for conducting focus groups, made a study of what people want and published it in his book, *What Americans Really Want... Really*. What he discovered is that the number one thing most people want is more money. However, what they wanted to do with more money varied greatly.

As I just mentioned, most of the people I asked didn't know what they wanted. However, when I pushed them for an answer they told me the kind of possessions they wanted, or the kind of vacation they wanted to take, or they told me they wanted to retire. That seems to agree with Luntz's findings. I'm sure some of them meant what they said but some of those responses were the result of marketing and advertisement; they had been influenced to say they wanted those things. Most of the things they told me they wanted were to please their five senses, and none of them defined the desire of their heart.

Suppose you get the things you think will make you happy but still don't know who you are or your GIFT. When you get a new car, a new house, a dream vacation, or retirement, how do you think you will feel? What need will those things fill? How long does the thrill of a new toy, or car or house, last? Do they satisfy the longing in your heart? Is that what you really desire?

> ## Once you know who you are and your GIFT, you will know your desire.

Once you know who you are and your GIFT, you will know your desire. You will desire to use your GIFT. If your GIFT, as determined by your CliftonStrengths assessment, is Maximizing, then you won't be happy unless you are maximizing something. If your GIFT is Activating, you will want to activate something or tell someone what to do (hopefully not your spouse). If your GIFT is Learning you won't be able to sit around doing nothing; you will have to find something to learn.

Knowing your identity is liberating because you can fulfill your desire. Until you experience the thrill of beginning to fulfill your desire you really haven't lived. That's why it is a common saying that most people go to the grave with their song still in them. I want you to sing your song. We all want to hear it. Of course, that doesn't work if you don't know your Special GIFT.

Passion

Have you ever met someone truly passionate about what they did? How did you feel when you were around them? I'll bet you weren't lukewarm. Passionate people either attract others or they repel them. There is usually no middle ground. Even if you are repelled by a passionate person, you might wish you had that same kind of emotion for something in your life.

It is passion that drives people over, under, around or through obstacles in their way. They intensely desire something, they know they have the GIFT to make it happen, and they are confident in the outcome. They keep going when passionless people would stop. To others, the person with passion appears to be superhuman. However, if you take a close look at the passionate person, there may be nothing about them that is superhuman. That is because desire and passion are spiritual assets. You can't see them, touch them, smell them, hear them, or taste them. But you know they are there.

Passion builds businesses, writes songs, paints masterpieces, attracts people, and lifts their spirits. Passion is the mother of invention. It helps you to endure and persist until you get what you desire. It also involves a strong emotion that is contagious and moving. We all want to be around passionate people.

Until I found my GIFT, I felt as if God had left the "passion chip" out of my design. I couldn't get passionate about anything even though I had been looking for something to put 100% of myself into since childhood. It seemed I was okay at most of the things I tried—from sports to music to schoolwork—but nothing made me want to go all in. To make things worse, my less than 100% effort was still better than most of my competition, so I was cruising through life "appearing" to be successful. The problem was that it wasn't good enough for me.

I have found that "good enough" keeps a lot of people from living with passion. It is just comfortable enough to keep them from finding their GIFT. Good is often the enemy of great.

> ## "Good enough" keeps people from living with passion. It is just comfortable enough to keep them from finding their GIFT.

I am fortunate to have cultivated a relationship with a very successful and passionate business leader and mentor, Jack. What's interesting is that my dad's name was also Jack, and he too was very passionate. Jack (my mentor) is focused and extremely self-disciplined, so much so that he can be intimidating if you don't know him. To me, his self-discipline appeared to take enormous effort and willpower, and to be honest I didn't know if I had that in me. Consequently, I wondered if I could ever be as passionate as him.

Jack introduced me to the success principles of Napoleon Hill. To be clear, I don't agree with everything Hill wrote, but he was closer to the mark on success than anyone else has been to this day. In *How to Raise Your Own Salary*, an obscure book written by Hill, he has a back and forth conversation with Andrew Carnegie. At one point, Carnegie says to Hill, *"obsessional desires make self-discipline very easy. It is no trouble at all to form thought-habits if one has a definite motive, backed by a strong emotional desire for the attainment of the object of the motive."*

In two sentences Hill described why I could not seem to get passionate about anything, and why self-discipline looked like such an overwhelming chore. I didn't know my desire. I have found that when you know who you are, find your GIFT, and discover your desire, you will realize two things: first, they have always been there; and second, passion always accompanies them.

Before I discovered this, I once asked Jack how I could find my passion. He just looked at me as if I were from outer space. The idea that someone didn't know their desire or wasn't passionate was foreign to him. Apparently, it was to Hill also because he doesn't tell you how to find your desire. He just said you need to know your desire before any of the success principles would work, which means pursuing your purpose without knowing your desire is worthless.

Can you imagine what the world would be like if even a fraction of the population knew their GIFT and were passionate about giving it? Think of the problems that would disappear overnight!

That's why I think finding your desire and living with passion is such a big deal. It really makes a difference!

Some Clues About Passion

Before I discovered my GIFT, even though I didn't know how to find my desire, there were moments when I was passionate. Those moments were clues. I remember attending a seminar in which the very passionate speaker said he woke up irritated every morning. I leaned over to my wife and whispered, "I can relate," to which she just shook her head in disapproval and said, "I know you can." Funny how a revelation to me was obvious to her. That's also a clue.

What the speaker made clear to me was that his daily irritated attitude was just part of his personality. It wasn't negative. It was how he was wired. That is exactly how I felt, but someone else had to express it before I realized the truth of the matter. Now, I needed to figure out why I was irritated and what caused it.

Some people become emotional more easily than others, so finding their passion may be a little bit easier. I don't get overly excited either positively or negatively, so the emotion I have is most often expressed as irritation. This is important because a key component of passion is a strong emotion. You will need to recognize how you express emotion to find your passion.

> # You will need to recognize how you express emotion to find your passion.

Finding your passion could be expressed through emotions of anger or agitation. It could be something that deeply disturbs you because no one is doing anything about it. It could be something that seems like injustice or a crime to you, or something that disturbs your sense of decency.

On the other hand, what you are passionate about could be something that warms your heart or makes you feel compassionate or loving. That is what I expected. I was greatly influenced by my father, who was both passionate and compassionate, so I expected my desire to be something that was more along the lines of charity work. The problem is that I am not wired that way.

If you find yourself asking why someone isn't doing something about what you feel emotional about, that's also a clue. You are probably the one who is supposed to do that "something." In fact, you are probably uniquely suited to do that "something" because you have the personality and GIFT to make it happen.

This all became clear to me while walking through a shopping mall one day. I saw a group of eighteen to twenty-year-olds hanging out together at this mall, which wasn't unusual at all. They weren't acting up or unruly, but what caught my attention was the way they were dressed. They were all dressed in black and were heavily tattooed, with more metal in their faces than a hardware store. My irritation at the sight quickly turned to anger, which isn't usual for me.

I didn't know why I felt that way, so I made myself do something very uncharacteristic. I went up and talked to them. At first, I noticed their eyes were dead, like nothing was going on inside, but as I started to talk to them I found they were nice kids. That's not what I expected.

I expected these Goths, as I later found out they were called, to be belligerent. That was not the case at all. I think they were grateful to speak to an adult in a normal conversation. What I found was that they were lost and had no idea of their potential. While most of the people I talked with wanted to make a difference, these kids didn't. They had given up on the world and didn't expect to amount to anything. That made me want to find their parents and smack them.

Here's what that trip to the mall showed me. The sight of those young people dressed in black got my attention and made me feel irritated. The irritation grew to an intense emotion when I spoke to them. All of this centered on how lost they were and that, unless something dramatically changed, these kids would have wasted lives. They had no clue how awesome they were or that they had a GIFT, and they certainly didn't seem to be looking for it. That bothered me. That's probably because I wasn't living up to my own potential either. The motivation behind my emotion was the irritation I felt, not a feeling of compassion for those poor lost souls.

What's funny is that the Goths didn't bother my wife a bit. That's another clue. If something makes you emotional but doesn't affect others as much as you, then you are probably the one that's supposed to do something about it. Mary is a health fanatic and she has been able to teach people to lose substantial amounts of weight and feel significantly better. When she sees an obese person or a woman with hormonal issues, she goes off! It really bothers her. Me, not so much.

Maybe you are one of those who gets irritated too, and your spouse or best friend doesn't understand why. What is it that gets you upset? (I don't mean people cutting you off in traffic; that ticks off everybody.) If you dig below the surface of the irritation, what is the underlying cause? On the other hand, maybe you are one that oozes with compassion for people over a special cause. Regardless of whether the emotion is love or anger, your intense emotion is an indication of your desire. You might have to get a little introspective, and it might be something that bothers you about yourself, but I'll bet you have a desire that could make a serious impact on that issue.

Confusion

Part of the reason that so many people don't identify their desire and they don't live with passion is that they use the wrong words. I have heard people use words like *goals, enthusiasm, motivation, self-discipline, desire,* and *passion* interchangeably as if they all meant the same thing. That's confusing, and it's not correct.

> When we try to succeed without desire and passion, our only option becomes to fail our way to success.

When we try to succeed without desire and passion (which is most often the case), our only option becomes trying to fail our way to success. Many success books talk about how important failure is in becoming successful. To fail your way to success you need:

- Self-discipline

- Enthusiasm

- Motivation

- Goals

- To be a Super Hero

The problem is that:

- Self-discipline is too much effort to do *forever*

- Enthusiasm always fades

- Motivation stops when the motivator is gone

- Goals are a poor substitute for PASSION

- Most of us ain't Super Heroes

Discipline (even self-discipline), enthusiasm, motivation, and goals are exerted from the outside. Either you or someone else *makes* you do something. On the other hand, desire and passion come from within. They are already there, trying to come out!

If you are told you *have to* do something that will require discipline, and you *must* hit certain goals, doesn't it sound like it is going to be difficult? If you are told you will need to go to training seminars to keep motivated, doesn't that tell you that what you will be doing won't be much fun? Yet, this is what a lot of us expect. We expect it to be hard, no fun, not exciting, and probably not too fulfilling. Without passion, the only way we can endure is by an outside force.

> ## Desire and passion come from within. They are already there trying to come out!

That is the problem with the First System described in Chapter 3. Trying to claw your way up the hierarchy of needs and out of the survival mode is not fun and may require super-human effort. If you don't have someone forcing you to do it, your chances of "making it" are not good. If all you know is the First System, and you aren't even aware that there is a Second System, you either decide to do the difficult or to just accept whatever comes your way.

Whenever you hear someone use words like "whatever," "another day, another dollar," or "it is what it is," you can tell they are working within the First System. Unfortunately, so are most of the people who sarcastically say "just living the dream." They don't know it is possible to live their dream, just not in the First System.

On the other hand, if you are planning to do something you desire and are passionate about, doesn't that sound like it would be exciting? If you put in long hours in pursuit of your desire, but it is something that gives you a lot of satisfaction, doesn't that beat a job where you watch the clock waiting to go home? What if you woke up every day excited to get back to doing the thing you love, with people who energize you? When this is your way of life, you may still have discipline and goals, but now they are a way of measuring where you are in respect to where you want to be. You really are "living the dream."

Enthusiasm can come and go, while *passion* lasts. Enthusiasm is a feeling or emotion that can be manufactured at will, and it can result in action, but that action is usually short-lived. Because enthusiasm can be created, it can also be manipulated. If enthusiasm is created but does not spring from passion, it will not get you the desire of your heart. It is interesting to note that other people will also be able to tell if your enthusiasm is manufactured or if it comes from passion.

In the movie *Master and Commander*, Russell Crowe plays the captain of an English warship during the Napoleonic Wars. A scene in the movie shows officers of the ship having dinner in the wardroom. Crowe's character, Captain Aubrey, was asked if he would tell an anecdote about Lord Admiral Nelson, a hero of the English Navy. Captain Aubrey said he had spoken with Nelson twice. "The second time he told me a story about how someone offered him a boat cloak on a cold night. He said, no, he didn't need it. He was quite warm. His zeal for king and country kept him warm."

As Aubrey looked around the dining table, he noticed the look of disbelief on the face of his friend, the ship's doctor. He continued, "I know it sounds absurd, and were it from another man, you would cry out, 'oh, what pitiful stuff' and dismiss it as **mere enthusiasm...**but with Nelson, you felt your heart glow."

In this scene, Captain Aubrey makes the point that there is a difference between mere enthusiasm and genuine passion. The difference is huge. The heart-glowing passion to do something great is what we all hope for. This is the kind of passion that drives one forward in the face of overwhelming odds. This is the kind of passion that seems obsessive to others. It does not know the word *defeat*. It is the kind of passion that allows one to go the extra mile, or even the extra ten miles, and do it with confidence and vigor. It is this kind of passion for a purpose that is the key to all great success.

> ## The heart-glowing passion to do something great is what we all hope for.

People with this kind of passion exude confidence, and yes...they can be enthusiastic. They have a contagious optimism and energy that stirs men's hearts. That is what Captain Aubrey felt as he stood next to Admiral Nelson on that cold night. That's why we go to movies; to see passion in heroes (action movies), in everyday lives (dramas), and romance (chick flicks).

Motivation is what we need to keep moving. Business leaders and sales managers will often go to great expense to orchestrate motivational events for their teams. They bring in motivational speakers to present emotional talks designed to "pump up" their staffs. They try to motivate them to get them back out on the trail, and to help them "keep on keeping on." These motivational events are designed to make sure they hit the next goal.

As we were preparing to leave the military and venture into the business world, my wife was introduced to the Amway business. Being a strong-willed leader of her own, she was quickly ushered in front of some of the top leadership in the organization to entice her to join their team.

The way I found out that "we" were in "the business" was during a long-distance call while I was on my last six-month military deployment in the Philippines. It was further explained when I arrived home. Being the intelligent man that I am, I went along with Mary's business ambitions to have a pleasant homecoming (you can read between the lines).

A couple of weeks after my homecoming, and after a two-day road trip, I found myself at a huge Amway conference in Spokane, Washington. I can tell you I wasn't really happy about using my military leave for a business meeting with a bunch of strangers, especially after having been deployed overseas for six months. All that changed once I got there. The meeting was electrifying and I wondered where these people had been all my life. They were speaking my language, and I was excited to get "our" business started.

Well, that enthusiasm lasted just about three months...just in time for the next big conference. Sure enough, I got all pumped up again, ready to tackle the world. And so, the cycle continued. The idea was to keep you motivated enough to keep working for three months to get some success under your belt.

To be honest, it worked for a while. We became moderately successful, obtaining what is called the Ruby level. However, I found myself relying on someone else to motivate me to build my own business instead of using my GIFT in my personality. What I found was that motivation is temporary, whereas passion endures.

Motivation is temporary, whereas passion endures.

Please do not hear what I am not saying. I am not saying that motivation, enthusiasm, or goals are bad things. What I am saying is that having enthusiasm, being motivated, or reaching for goals without desire and passion will only give you very temporary results. If you are passionate about your desire, you won't need anyone to pump you up. If you are truly passionate about what you are doing, you will naturally be enthusiastic, and everyone around you will know it.

If someone must set goals for you, and then manages you to make sure you hit them, it is a sure sign you are not passionate about what you are doing. All the books and management theories about goal-setting were written to make people do things for which they do not have a desire or passion. Those books and management theories were probably written by people who have high **D**-style personalities. High **D** personalities can make themselves do things they don't want to do by giving themselves a swift (mental) kick in their rear ends. If you are not a high **D** personality, and you could hear the self-talk of one of these Dominant, Directing Doers, it would probably scare you to death.

Even the **D** personalities can't force themselves to hit goals forever. They burn out too. They only *appear* to be successful without knowing their desires. Anyone who does not know what they desire in their lives will have a huge hole in their heart. Anyone who is driven by something other than passion, but especially **D** personalities, can make a lot of people unhappy. That is because without purpose and passion abuse is inevitable, and **D**s don't tend to do things halfway.

> ## Passion feeds causes, fuels vision, builds businesses, rights injustices, creates beauty, and is the source of compassion.

Passion feeds causes, fuels vision, builds businesses, rights injustices, creates beauty, and is the source of compassion. Without passion, people just go through the motions and try to survive. Without passion, a normal response to a challenge is "whatever." I hate that reply. It is dead, unemotional, uncaring, without thought, and apathetic. That is no way to go through life. People do want to find something they are passionate about and can devote their lives to; their purpose.

Recap

Before we move on, this is a good place to recap a few things.

1. **Who you really are**

   You are a unique, one-of-a-kind person. Many factors combine to make you who you really are; probably the most important is your personality. You have had your personality from birth, it is perfect for you, and it will help to unlock the door to your GIFT. Why would you guess as to your personality when there is a simple, painless, and fun DISC assessment you can take so you can know?

Who you are is also shaped by your Father Fracture (we all have one to some degree), which generation you are part of, your gender, how you think about money, and how you give and receive love.

2. You have a Special GIFT

More than just what you do, it is your unique way of thinking and making a difference. Your GIFT is more than a skill, an ability, an aptitude, or a talent. How you think is what separates you from everyone else, and what enables you to achieve greatness.

There is an assessment that will help you to determine your GIFT. The CliftonStrengths assessment will provide your top five strengths, in order, the first of which I call your GIFT. The odds of someone else having the same assessment as yours are astronomical. Your GIFT is special, and it is the Master Key to your desire, your purpose, and to making a difference.

You will not be able to discover your Special GIFT until you know who you really are.

3. You will naturally desire to use your Special GIFT

Your desire is your *"Want To"*—a strong internal intention sustained by the capacity to endure. The desire of your heart is always related to your GIFT. You will naturally desire to use your GIFT, and this leads to passion. You can't manufacture desire; you were born with it.

Chapter 9
Make a Difference

Napoleon Hill, the famed author of *Think and Grow Rich*, *The Law of Success*, and several other books on success, says that he began his quest to make a difference after speaking with Andrew Carnegie in an interview. Carnegie charged Hill with the task of compiling a success philosophy that would benefit mankind and then introduced Hill to the wealthiest people in America. Hill studied these people for twenty years and then published his findings on their common principles in *The Law of Success*.

As written by Hill, Carnegie said the most important principle of success is to have a Definite Major Purpose. Since I didn't have one of those (a Definite Major Purpose), finding my purpose became my quest. As I began talking to people about purpose I quickly discovered that the whole concept of purpose scared most people, so I changed my questions.

Instead of asking people about their purpose, I started to ask people what they really wanted. Surprisingly, most of the people I talked with did not know what they wanted. They were cruising through life, hoping for the best. Some had a plan of sorts, but they couldn't define what they wanted. If I pushed them for an answer, the most common response was that they wanted to make a difference. But what does that mean?

Making a difference means
doing something important that helps people or
makes the world a better place.

The idiom *to make a difference* means doing something important that helps people or makes the world a better place, according to the dictionary. That didn't help me a bit, so I did an internet search with the keywords "make a difference." That led me to believe that almost anything can be spun into somehow making a difference, and much of what I found on the internet was pretty weird.

Of course, this isn't new. Almost every generation has done some pretty weird things in their search for significance...which reminds me of a movie I once watched—okay, I watched it about twenty times. It is about knights going on a quest (a long, arduous search) for the holy grail. Their search to make a difference was called *Monty Python and the Holy Grail.*

In Monty Python's version of King Arthur's quest, Arthur and a handful of his knights approached the Bridge of Death. If they could cross that bridge, they believed they would find the Holy Grail. To pass over the bridge, they first had to contend with a horrible old man named the "Bridge Keeper."

If Arthur and his knights could answer the Bridge Keeper's questions, he would allow them to cross the bridge, but if they failed to answer all three questions correctly, they would die by being cast into a deep gorge. The first knight answered his questions with no problem. The second knight wasn't so lucky. After stumbling on the third question (about his favorite color), he was tossed into the gorge. When King Arthur's turn came to answer the Bridge Keeper, the scene went something like this:

Bridge Keeper: Who would cross the Bridge of Death must answer me these questions three, ere the other side he see. What is your name?

Arthur: Arthur, King of the Britons.

Bridge Keeper: What is your quest?

Arthur: To seek the Holy Grail.

Bridge Keeper: What is the airspeed velocity of an unladen swallow?

Arthur: An African or European swallow?

Bridge Keeper: I don't know that...oooooooh.... (The Bridge Keeper himself was flung to his death in the deep gorge.)

Then, Sir Galahad asked King Arthur, as they crossed over the Bridge of Death, "How do you know so much about swallows?"

Arthur: You have to know these things when you are king.

The movie is very funny, but that is not why I mention it. There are a couple of points I would like to make from this scene. First, I didn't know the answer to a very basic question: "What do you seek?" Neither did most of the people I asked. Maybe because, as a quest, it sounded like it was a long, arduous journey to find the answer. Asking people if they wanted to make a difference sounded much less arduous, so I changed my question.

The second point to be made from King Arthur's meeting with the Bridge Keeper is that Arthur knew who he was. He didn't just answer "Arthur", but said he was king of the Britons. His answer left no doubt as to who he was.

So, what's the point? I'm glad you asked! The point is:

1. To make a difference,
     you need to know your purpose.

2. To know your purpose,
     you need to know your gift.

3. To know your gift,
     you need to know who you really are.

What Does It Mean to Make a Difference?

Making a difference means different things to different people. Remembering that the definition of making a difference is *to do something important.* What is important to you?

If you don't know your Special GIFT you could answer this question in many different ways. You could want to…

- Save the world

- Cure poverty

- Start a foundation

- Enter a ministry

- Run for political office

- Provide for your family

- Invent something life-changing

- Create a business

If you are trapped in the basic needs part of Maslow's Hierarchy, your idea of making a difference might mean having a good meal or finding an apartment you can afford. Since the number one thing most people want is more money, then making a difference to them means having enough money to do more than merely surviving.

A *Forbes* magazine article from January 2016 said that 63% of Americans don't have enough savings to cover a $500 emergency. So, a note of realism needs to be applied to the concept of what is most important to you and how you want to make a difference. You might hope to do something great someday, but that extra $500 would really make a difference now. That being said, finding your GIFT can make a direct impact on your income, which, in turn, can affect how you can make a difference.

Making a Difference =
Purpose + Desire, applied to a Vision or Cause.

Making a difference involves knowing your Purpose and Desire, and applying them to a Vision or a Cause. This is precisely the point where most people become frustrated. They may want to make a difference but they don't know their purpose or their desire, they don't have a vision, and the only cause they are concerned about is the $500 emergency we just mentioned. So, if that's you, please hold on. There is hope.

You could also think that your ability to make a difference is all up to you. You could think that you are going to have to make a difference all by yourself. That is rarely the case. If you happen to be one of those rare people with a vision or you are the one ambitious enough to start a cause, then your GIFT could be the most important part of the cause. However, you will still need other people and their GIFTs to make your vision or cause a reality. Since most people are not visionaries, their GIFTs are meant to combine with the GIFTs of others to make those visions reality. So, you see, it is not all up to you.

Then there are those who are deluded into thinking that as long as they are doing something, anything, important that it will make a difference. It is possible that doing legitimately important work can make a difference, but it will never make as big a difference and offer you the same satisfaction as using your GIFT.

Another misconception is that if you just belong to something important, it will make a difference. You could hear of a good cause that appeals to you emotionally. Before you know it, you are involved and you may even be doing a good work, but you are not fulfilled. That is because you can belong to a good cause and not fulfill your purpose. A friend worked in a large ministry in a Chicago suburb, doing great work to increase the size and scope of the ministry. The problem was that he wasn't using his GIFT and his personal growth was stifled.

He found that he had to leave this ministry before he could make a difference.

So, a lot of people talk about making a difference, but few do. Regardless of how you want to make a difference it still holds that:

1. To make a difference, you need to know your purpose.

2. To know your purpose, you need to know your gift.

3. To know your gift, you need to know who you really are.

The good news is that these are all possible!

Chapter 10

Operating in Your Special GIFT

Brad was a handsome twenty-four-year-old, came from a good family, and seemed to have things going his way. Even so, as the middle of four children, Brad (not his real name) was the one who didn't quite fit in. His three sisters were all high-achieving, gregarious college graduates, but not Brad. He was a quiet, reserved young man who struggled through high school and did not attend college.

Brad's parents were loving and hard-working. They tried to do whatever they could for all of their children, but wondered what went wrong with their parenting of Brad. They could not figure out what his dilemma was or how to help him. The more they tried the further he seemed to slip away.

Brad loved his parents and sisters but just couldn't relate to them. His personality was nothing like theirs, so communication became difficult. To fit in somewhere, he resorted to hanging out with "friends," who introduced him to drugs. Things became so strained with his family that he finally moved out of their house and took a menial job in a nearby city.

Brad was just drifting until he came home one fateful Thanksgiving. His mom had recently purchased several copies of *The Joe Purpose Master Key: 7 Steps to Making a Difference by Finding Your Purpose* for her business associates. She gave a book to Brad, not thinking that he would read it. Something about the book caught Brad's attention and he didn't just read it, he devoured it. He purchased the assessments recommended in the book, even though he was short on cash, and started to learn who he was.

Brad began to realize that his way of thinking was dramatically different from anyone in his family. He discovered why they had a difficult time communicating and why he felt so out of place.

Once he found out that his creativity and soft spirit were perfectly suited to his GIFT, Brad started to feel good about himself. It is difficult to love yourself if you don't know yourself, and if you don't love yourself you can't love anyone else. This can be especially frustrating for a naturally loving person like Brad.

Brad's story is one of a person who did not learn well in the world's education system, but who began consuming books that would help him to be a success. He started to apply this new knowledge and began making a career for himself. Finding his GIFT and beginning to operate in it made Brad appear to be a whole new person. It is very probable that he would never have known he had a Special GIFT if he hadn't read about it, and he attributed his dramatic change to a book his mother gave him at Thanksgiving.

The Stapler and the Hammer

The most precious gift anyone has received is life. Without being born, any discussion about purpose or the future would be pointless. You had no control over where, when, how, or to whom you were born. It was a gift.

The second most precious gift anyone has received is the ability to think. The ability to use reason, reflect, and meditate as part of one's mental process is what I mean by thinking, and only humans can do that. In addition, no two people think the same way. The way in which you form thoughts and your brain's neural pathways are unique to you. Your very unique way of thinking is what I call your Special GIFT. Again, I capitalize GIFT to differentiate it from all other gifts.

The challenge with this concept of your unique way of thinking being a Special GIFT is that we have not been trained to use it. Instead we are educated by a system that trains everyone to think like everyone else, and are considered abnormal if we don't. That is what Brad discovered in the previous section. However, it is your uniqueness that is the Master Key to unlocking all the success for which you were created. Using your Special GIFT leads to satisfaction in what you do, creativity in your work, and the financial and the personal success you long for.

> # Using your Special GIFT leads to satisfaction in what you do, creativity in your work, and the financial success you long for.

We have been told that if we get the right education and if we put in enough hard work, we can be as successful as we want. We have been trained to achieve the success that society chooses, and marketed to by advertising companies to reinforce their descriptions of success.

To prove my point, think for a few moments about the things you would like to have, and what achieving success would look like to you. This isn't necessarily a bad thing, but most of us would consider a certain kind of house, the "right "spouse," your kids' college paid for, the right vacations, a certain amount of money in the bank, and a secure retirement as being a definition of success. Again, there is nothing wrong with any of those things, but did you choose those or were you trained to think that was correct by society?

To help make my point, imagine for a moment that you aren't a person, but you are a tool. You are a stapler—the kind of stapler you might find on a desk in an office. Imagine further that you need to get a job. Maybe you have bills to pay and you are looking for a new career with a better income.

You find out that the ACME Company is hiring and you decide to apply for a position. The problem is that they are looking for someone with experience as a hammer. You have been used to hammer nails in walls to hang up pictures, and your dad is a sledgehammer, so you know the hammer kind of language. Since you really want this job you list experience as a hammer on your resume even though you are a stapler.

The ACME Company Human Resources person at your interview is very nice, and asks you a bunch of standard questions. You handle all the questions well, get along with the people you met at the company, and then go home to wait for a response. About a week later you get a call from ACME Company, asking you when you can start. Yippee, you are hired!

Your first day at ACME Company is taken up with filling out paperwork. The second day they take you on a tour of the company and introduce you to your new supervisor. He "sort of" fills you in on what they do and what he thinks you are supposed to do. He also introduces you to your co-workers and tells you to be back tomorrow at eight o'clock to get started. There is no job description and there are no other hammers in the company, but you don't give it too much thought. You are excited to start your new career.

After a few months on the job, you begin to wonder if you made the right choice. Being a hammer means pounding on things, which is not natural to you and it is taking a toll on you. You feel beat up and out of place. No one else seems to notice, so maybe you are doing all right and just need a little more time. But something in the back of your mind tells you this isn't what you are supposed to do. Sure, the pay is better, and you have something to talk to your father about, but being a hammer is hard work. They want you to do stuff you have no idea how to do, they don't give you any instruction, and they get angry with you when you don't hammer things the way they expect.

All the time you are at work you can't help thinking about how cool it would be to put pieces of paper together. When you see a stack of paper that is fastened with a paper clip you just know there is a better way. Whenever you see loose paper flying around the room it bothers you. You wonder why no one does anything about it. Then reality sets in and it is back to work banging things into a wall. Is it five o'clock yet? Is it Friday?

The Morals of the Story

1. Many of us are acting as hammers when we are really staplers. We'll accept a job for which we aren't suited because we think it is the right thing to do. If our goal is to make more money, accumulate the trapping of success, and someday be able to retire, then putting up with a job as a hammer is okay if it gets you there. However, if your goal is to find your purpose and achieve what you were born to achieve, anything short of being the best stapler just won't do.

2. Denying your true identity will leave you feeling out of sorts and unfulfilled. Even if you make a lot of money as a hammer, you won't realize your purpose until you become the stapler you were born to be. The truth is that without purpose, abuse is inevitable— meaning if you use something in a way it was not intended, there will be consequences. In the Stapler and the Hammer story, eventually, the stapler is going to break. In real life, something in your life will be abused if you don't apply your GIFT. This causes all kinds of problems with stress, relationships, depression, and other health-related issues. Maybe that's why health care benefits are such a big deal...the wrong jobs are killing us.

3. The ACME Company cannot tell a hammer from a stapler. Most companies hire based on the experience of the candidate. They rarely consider the GIFT of the person being hired. As long as the position gets filled and the task that position requires gets done, they are happy. They are hiring someone to fulfill a task, not create solutions for potential problems. If you are hired as a hammer, most companies don't want to hear your solutions for loose paper flying around a room. If you aren't a good enough hammer, they will just replace you with someone else.

4. You can make your resume say whatever you want when applying for a position, but it won't end well. It is always more fulfilling and more rewarding to be who you really are. This means you need to know you are a stapler, be able to communicate that to others and tell them your value to the organization. You need to know you have a Special GIFT before you can ever use it.

> # It is always more fulfilling and more rewarding to be who you really are.

Talent vs. GIFT

In Chapter 6 we discussed what a Special GIFT is and how your top talent from the CliftonStrengths assessment from Gallup (formerly known as StrengthsFinder) is what I call your Special GIFT. To operate in your Special GIFT requires understanding how that top talent works in combination with your other talents from the assessment. (Side note: Gallup says what they actually measure is talent, not strengths, even though they call it a strengths assessment.)

Taking the assessment will give you the results of your thirty-four talents listed in order from highest to lowest based on your answers to the questions in the assessment. You can also get an abbreviated readout of just your top five talents, which is sufficient for most people. These results are helpful in two ways. First, they prove how unique your particular way of thinking is. The chances that someone else has the same five talents as you, and in the same order, is one in thirty-three million, and the chances that someone has all thirty-four talents in the same order as yours is infinite. Your way of thinking is unique to you alone.

The second way that your results are helpful is understanding the importance of the order of your top five talents. For example, your top talent (GIFT) could be Activator, as is my wife, Mary's. She naturally wants to make things happen by turning thoughts into action. She can't help it. Whenever she walks into a company she immediately begins evaluating how to make things happen by telling people what to do. She convinces people of their abilities and gets them moving.

Many other people have the same top talent (Activator) as Mary. What makes her GIFT unique is what she applies her top talent to. That is largely determined by the next four talents listed in the results of her assessment.

Mary's top five strengths are:

1. Activator

2. Relator

3. Competition

4. Belief

5. Responsibility

Her second strength is Relator. This means that she wants to activate people. Her plainspoken manner, her strong sense of belief, and the fact that she takes responsibility for her actions results in people constantly seeking her advice. Without having to think about it, she tells them what to do, and amazingly to me, they just do it. It is her GIFT!

What if Mary's second talent was Futuristic and her third talent was Strategic? She would probably want to activate a project that dealt with something long term or that she was convinced was going to happen in the future. Additionally, this order of talents would mean she would be working on—actually getting others to work on—plans to make it happen. That is very different from an Activator with Relator as a second talent.

Let's go back to the story of the stapler and the hammer. The stapler's GIFT was to be a stapler, not a hammer. Operating in his GIFT as a stapler depended on a few other things. Would he staple a few sheets of paper as part of a kit of other office supplies for someone who travels? Then he might be a compact stapler with just a few staples, perfect for small jobs. Would he be an industrial stapler, assembling books of one hundred pages or more? Then he might be a large, heavy-duty stapler powered by electricity. Or maybe he would be a versatile desk stapler for use in an office. In each case, the GIFT is a stapler, but the way it operates is determined by other factors.

Saint Paul talked about the same thing when he spoke about gifts in his first letter to the Corinthians some two thousand years ago. He said there was a variety of gifts, a variety of ministries, and a variety of effects. The same gift could be used in different ministries for different effects.

He went on to describe how the parts of a body work together as an illustration of how gifts were designed to work. According to Paul, no one gift was better than another and each gift was necessary for the body to work as intended. He compared gifts to body parts like one's eye, or nose, or ear, or foot. He said we shouldn't all want to have the same gift, even if we thought of it as being more appealing or attractive. What would a body be if all the parts were eyes? This was clearly to tell us not to try to be what we are not.

Each part of the body is needed for the body to work. Even if you have a GIFT similar to someone else, it may be needed in a different area to achieve a different result. Likewise, your GIFT may be the same top talent as someone else, but how you choose to operate in that GIFT, based on your other talents, may be different.

Any way you look at it, operating in your GIFT means understanding your top talent and how your other talents support it. Your top talent describes the overarching way that you think. I think like a Maximizer and my wife thinks like an Activator. What I want to Maximize and what Mary wants to Activate are determined by the other four talents of our assessments. They provide a very accurate description of how we naturally think and want to operate.

GIFT or Experience

The most common way for someone to try to apply their Special GIFT is in a career. This means you intend to work in a company that will pay you for your work. You probably want to do something that makes a difference, with other people you like, and for a salary that takes care of more than you need. But what does the company want? What criteria do the Human Resource people and your future boss look at to decide if they will hire you? Do they look at your resume to determine your Special GIFT or do they resort to determining if you have relevant experience for the job?

Most companies do not know what they want in a job candidate.

I researched what companies look for in candidates for potential jobs, and the results were very interesting. My conclusion is that most companies, especially small to midsize companies, do not know what they want in a candidate. They often can't even give you a description of the position they want to be filled. They just know they are too busy, and they need someone else to help take the load off. The result is that they end up looking for work experience that comes close to what they have in mind.

Because they are already overwhelmed and desperately need help, they have no time to train new employees. Training puts a drain on the resources they have, which are already stretched too thin, so the company wants someone that can occupy a seat and get started as fast as possible with minimal training or supervision.

The company that is looking to hire you probably assumes you already know what you want. They want you to apply the skills you have already learned somewhere else (through experience) to their problems. They are not interested in teaching you new skills or helping you to figure out how to apply your GIFT to their particular product or service.

They expect you to do that. Your skill in performing a particular task is what they want to pay you for, and your income depends on how much value they place on that task. Your income does not depend on how much value they place on you. If you can be replaced at a lower cost to the company...guess what?

So, what does this have to do with applying your Special GIFT and operating in it? First, you need to understand the reality of your value to a company based on your experience. Unless you have very unique experience, you will probably be replaceable. Second, most companies are more familiar with skills than they are GIFTS. Skills are what are used to accomplish particular tasks, but GIFTS are applied to a vision.

If the company you work for, or are hoping to work for, does not have a vision, then they will not appreciate your Special GIFT and this will not be a place for you to fulfill your purpose. While experience can be important, employing your Special GIFT is your purpose, and operating in it is what makes a difference.

Vision

Making a difference is applying the special and unique way you think, based on who you are, to what you desire in a vision or a cause. If the company you are contemplating working for does not have a cause or a vision, you will need to look elsewhere to make a difference.
You were born with your GIFT and your desire. As you begin to realize

who you really are, those facts become more evident. Then, as you start to use your GIFT, you will discover that whatever you apply your GIFT to will have to involve other people. No one can make a difference by themselves; it will always require other people.

Whether you call it a cause, a mission, a ministry, a movement, or a vision, you will have to be a part of something bigger than yourself to make a difference.

I refer to that something as a vision, and it needs to be defined so that you will understand what I am trying to say. By vision, I don't mean sight, and I don't mean a dream. A vision is a clear, long-term direction that can be concisely communicated, and that inspires others to be a part of or follow.

> A vision is a clear, long-term direction that can be concisely communicated, and that inspires others to be a part of or follow.

Visions are created by visionaries. These are people who look to the future and see things as they can be, not as they are. Visionaries are the sources of all real progress and are usually charismatic, creative, and uplifting. They exhort people and organizations to reach their full potential. Visionaries can create their own organizations to fulfill their vision, or they can take an organization that exists and breathe new life into it. They say things like "what if?", "why not?", and "just imagine."

While individuals have a purpose for their lives, visionaries have visions for organizations. Everyone has a purpose but not everyone has a vision. Visionaries have visions. However, everyone should be part of a vision because that is where your GIFT will make a difference.

> # Visions are created by visionaries. Everyone has a purpose but not everyone has a vision.

WARNING! Don't be fooled by an organization with a vision statement: that doesn't necessarily mean they have a vision. Many organizational vision statements were created by a business consultant because the owner thought their organization should have one. They are often written, disseminated throughout the company, and then promptly forgotten.

Wisely choosing an organization to be a part of is very important. You should know the purpose of the organization and its vision. I once hired some former military members to be part of a sales team. In a training session for the team, I asked them what the purpose of business was, and was surprised at their answers. Most of them thought the purpose of a business was to provide jobs for people.

Well, that explained a lot about their attitudes and why most of them had to be replaced. In case you are wondering, the purpose of any business is to make a profit. If it doesn't make a profit it goes out of business, and if an employee doesn't help the company make a profit they won't stay employed for long. Most companies know their purpose, as do most organizations. You need to know them as well.

In choosing an organization to be a part of, you need to know both its purpose and its vision. We already discussed the purpose of business, but there are other types of organizations. What is the purpose of an educational organization? What is the purpose of a nonprofit? What's the purpose of your church or ministry? Do you want to be part of something really big, or do you prefer a smaller and more intimate setting? Are you motivated by money, by accomplishment, or something else? Your choice depends on who you are, your GIFT, and your desire.

Most organizations know their purpose, but relatively few have a vision. That is because most organizations are managed and very few are led. Managers manage assets and often regard employees as assets that can be replaced. They look at their labor costs as part of their bottom line. A profitable company can be the result of good management, with or without leadership and vision. It can be a place for you to receive a paycheck, but probably not a place to fulfill your purpose or make a difference.

Leaders lead people. Leadership involves inspiring others to fulfill a vision, and most visionaries also possess leadership traits. They encourage their employees to fulfill their potential because their GIFTs are vital to the vision. Visionary leaders can be found in many different fields. You can find visionaries in politics, in sports, in religion, in business, in education, and in many other fields. In each case, they inspire people rather than using fear and threats to get them to do things. These leaders know where they are going and they find people who want to go in the same direction. You will know when you find a visionary leader.

The point is that if you are not a visionary, which most people are not, then you need to find a vision you want to be a part of. That is where your purpose should be applied, and that is how you will make a difference. Choosing the wrong vision will lead to disappointment and disillusion. Choosing the right vision will allow you to use your GIFT and make the difference you have always wanted.

> ## The vision you want to be a part of will speak to your heart more than to your head.

The vision you want to be a part of will speak to your heart more than to your head. It will be something you feel proud of and will want to tell others about. Even if your friends and family don't understand what you are so enthusiastic about, it won't matter because it is your purpose being fulfilled, not theirs.

The vision you want to belong to could be a way for you to right a wrong or injustice you feel strongly about. It could be that the vision allows you to unleash your creativity as part of something bigger. It could be a way for you to create large amounts of income, or just to live modestly. Your part in the vision could be in the limelight, or it could be a supporting role. Regardless, you know that your GIFT is a valuable part of the overall vision, and you know that your valuable GIFT makes a difference.

I heard it put this way: jobs are temporary assignments until you find your work. You can retire from a job and you can be fired from a job because a job just pays your bills. Your work is what you were meant to do. Your work is what you do with your Special GIFT. You can never be fired from your work, nor do you retire from it. You should be looking to do your work as part of the right vision. You were given your personality, your desire, and your GIFT for a reason. Your place in the right vision does exist, and you will find it.

> ## "Jobs are temporary assignments until you find your work."
> ### Myles Monroe

Lead or Follow

There is an age-old debate over whether leaders are born or made. Those who believe that leaders can be made will say that anyone can be trained to lead, or that people rise to leadership based on the situation. On the other hand, those who believe that leaders are born will acknowledge that people can be in "leadership roles" without being natural leaders, but the real leaders are born that way. Part of this debate is because we have elevated leadership to such a high level that being a follower is considered inferior. Not so! Can you imagine if everyone was a leader? It would be chaos.

> # We have elevated leadership to such a high level that being a follower is considered inferior. Not so!

I define a leader as someone who possesses these four traits:

1. **A leader knows who they are.**
   - They **know** their Identity and their GIFT.

2. **A leader knows the GIFTs of others.**
   - They **know** the Identities and GIFTs of those who work for them.
   - They place them in the best positions based on their GIFTs.

3. **A leader believes in and is able to communicate a vision.**
   - A vision is the direction an organization is headed and the expected outcome of heading that way. It is a mental image of what the future will be like.
   - The vision may not necessarily be their own vision.
   - **A leader without vision (their own or someone else's) is a manager**. This is not derogatory.

4. **A leader inspires others to follow the vision.**
   - The leader gives clear direction to followers.
   - The leader leads by example.

- The leader exhorts and encourages followers to be their best.

As you can tell, I don't believe everyone is a leader. Most of us are followers in search of a visionary leader. A lot has been written about leadership in business, in the military, in sports, in politics, and in church. It is directed at telling potential leaders how to get an existing group of people to do something. How well you get them to do what you want determines what kind of leader you are. These books and articles are always written to or for the "leader."

But what do followers have to say about leaders? *Strengths Based Leadership* by Tom Rath and Barry Conchie published findings based on a 2005-2008 study of followers. What they found out is not what "leaders" expected. Followers did not describe leaders with words like:

- vision

- purpose

- charisma

- dynamic speaker

- wisdom

- humor

Those are the kinds of words that leaders used.

The words that followers chose to describe leaders they follow were words like:

- trust

- compassion

- stability

- hope

Followers trust leaders they have known for a long time. They have seen them act in all kinds of situations and trust they will make the right decisions. They know the leader cares about them as people and they aren't just assets or a bottom-line expense. Followers feel their leader is stable when he or she is transparent and can be counted upon, and they want their leader to give them hope for a bright future.

The point is that there are leaders and there are followers. Relatively few people are leaders, so that makes most people followers. One is not better than the other. If you don't know which you are, a leader or a follower, it will be very difficult to make a difference. A leader who tries to "fit in" ends up becoming frustrated and probably disruptive to the organization. That is because leaders don't fit in; they lead. A follower who is trying to be a leader will become equally frustrated, probably wondering why no one is following. They usually result to using force rather than inspiration to keep their subordinates in line.

When you recognize your place in an organization as either a leader or a follower, it gives you more confidence in using your GIFT. It will also allow others in the organization to use their GIFTs in a spirit of harmony. Leaders use their GIFTs to provide vision, direction, and inspiration. Followers use their GIFTs for everything else.

> ## Each person fits into a vision naturally, not by trying harder.

If you find yourself constantly having to prove yourself to others, you may be acting in the wrong role. Each person fits into a vision naturally, not by trying harder. If you feel like a square peg trying to fit in a round hole, part of the problem is that you may be a follower who is trying to lead or a leader who is trying not to rock the boat by attempting to fit in. Leaders lead…all the time. Followers follow.

Choosing a Career

On a practical level, operating in your Special GIFT probably means choosing the right career within the right organization. Whether your career is a business, a job in someone else's business, or a ministry, choosing the right career will be a big factor in whether you make a difference or not.

Regardless of your situation, the steps are the same. The master key to finding your career is to discover your Special GIFT. The biggest reason that people don't find their Special GIFT (besides not taking the CliftonStrengths assessment from Gallup) is that they don't know who they are, and the biggest reason they don't know who they are is that they have a Father Fracture.

Once you know your Special GIFT you will be able to discover what you desire. You will desire to use your GIFT, which is another way to define your purpose. It is your choice whether you decide to follow and develop your purpose, and if you do it will begin to turn into passion. Applying that passion to a cause or vision that you care about is the best way to choose a career.

But what if you don't have all the pieces of the puzzle yet? What if you are just graduating from high school or college and you don't know where to look for causes or have the life experiences to help you figure this out? Taking the personality assessment and strengths assessment as recommended in the *What's Next?* section will certainly help. I would also recommend exposing yourself to as many possible choices as possible so that you will be aware of potential careers.

Some people under the age of twenty-five say that they have too many choices and possible directions they can go. They have a difficult time choosing because they are afraid of making the wrong choice. There is a scientific reason for that. The human brain is not fully developed until one is twenty-five years old. It takes that long for the frontal cortex (the portion of the brain responsible for reasoned thinking) to develop. Until that time, one's brain functions more on emotion.

I had no idea that was the case when I left college and entered the Marine Corps. I can tell you that my decisions about a career were based more on a romantic notion of what it would be like to be a military pilot than on any amount of reasoning. Early in my career I was glad to be exposed to all kinds of people, from all walks of life, and to be able to coordinate the efforts of multiple career fields to accomplish missions. In my twelve years as a Marine officer, I had at least twelve different jobs in addition to my primary role as a pilot. That was not unusual. I had no idea what a great learning experience I was receiving as a young adult in the military. That helps to explain why many companies like to recruit former military people—they can make more informed choices than people with comparatively fewer experiences.

If you are unsure of what career to choose, then the military may be a good place for you to go to help figure this out. There are other agencies and organizations that can serve the same function. My point is that you don't have to agonize over making sure you get it right the first time you accept a career. Changing jobs until you find your purpose may be necessary.

On the other hand, you may have already chosen a career field and be well down the path. You may have followed the advice of a parent, a teacher, or someone else and now you are in a career that does not use your Special GIFT. Some people in this situation stay trapped in their career because they are wearing "golden handcuffs." They are making a good income, and even though they don't like what they do, the risk of changing direction keeps them handcuffed to their job. If that is your predicament you will need some kind of a catalyst to encourage you to live with purpose rather than stay handcuffed to a job you dislike.

Whether you are under twenty-five years old and looking for the right career or you are already down the path in the wrong career, you have another choice that may work for you. Rather than boldly starting from scratch and risking your income, you can make money doing something else, even if you don't like it, while you develop your GIFT. When you get to the point where your income from using your Special GIFT exceeds your other income, your decision to dedicate yourself to your purpose should be easy.

But there is a trap with that path. It can be very easy to become lulled into complacency while you develop your GIFT. The danger is that your job and its income may be just good enough to distract you from the greatness that comes from operating in your Special GIFT. The fulfillment you will receive from employing your Special GIFT in a vision is well worth the effort. Even though "good enough" may feel all right, fulfilling your purpose is your destiny. You will never feel content until you operate in your Special GIFT.

Chapter 11
Benefits of Knowing Your GIFT

If I am going to propose you change your life to one centered around your Special GIFT rather than trying to succeed in life by continually updating skills for a job that just makes money, then there needs to be a reason for you to do so. There are many benefits of knowing and using your Special GIFT, and I created an acronym to help you remember them.

The acronym comes from an old television show. Some of my earliest memories are of going to the beach in Puerto Rico. My father was stationed at Roosevelt Roads Naval Base, and life near the ocean was great for an active kid. Consequently, my favorite television shows at that time were all about the ocean. One of those shows was about Jacques Cousteau's ocean exploration and the other was called *Flipper*. Flipper was about two boys and their adventures with a dolphin named Flipper.

FLIPPER

FLIPPER is the acronym I use for the benefits of knowing your Special GIFT. It stands for:

- Faithfulness

- Love

- Income

- Passion

- Purpose

- Excellence

- Relationship

Faithfulness

My family coat of arms has the motto *Ad Finem Fidelis*, which means *faithful to the end*. Additionally, being a former Marine, the motto *Semper Fidelis*, which means *always faithful*, holds a special place to me. So, the whole idea of faith has meant something special to me for most of my life. The question is, faith in or to what?

Faith is defined as having complete trust or confidence in someone or something. That can represent a real problem for most of us today. Having complete trust in someone or something inevitably leads to disappointment. Institutions that we thought were trustworthy have proven otherwise with alarming regularity. Can you really say you trust the government or the church, or even your company, to always do the right thing? And whenever you completely trust another person, no matter how good they might be, they will surely let you down at some point. That is because no one is completely trustworthy, not even you.

> ## Your GIFT is the special way that God designed you to succeed on earth.

So then, how can faithfulness be a benefit of knowing your GIFT? Your Special GIFT was given specifically to you by God when you were created. Trusting in your GIFT to succeed in life, rather than in what other people or institutions tell you, requires faith. Your GIFT is the special way that God designed you to succeed on earth. Remaining faithful to developing and employing your GIFT will give you much more sustainable success than whatever you may have trusted in the past.

Love

Love is one of the most misunderstood words in the English language. We use the same word to mean many different things. You could say "I love you," which means something different from "I love chocolate," which means something different from "I love America," which means something different from "love one another as I have loved you."

That is because we use one word for the same thing that is described by at least four different words in Greek (the language of the New Testament of the Bible). The Greek language used these words for different aspects of love:

> *Eros*—This the romantic, intimate, erotic kind of love. It usually refers to the physical love of the body.

> *Stergo*—This describes the love for one's family, community, or country.

> *Phileo*—This is the love between equals such as in friendship or brotherly love.

> *Agape*—This describes a selfless and unconditional love.

When you employ your GIFT, you will notice that it will have these attributes: it will be a joy; you'll be peaceful about it (no striving); you will be patient, kind, and gentle with those you are giving it to; you'll know what you are doing is good; and you will naturally have self-control as you give. You won't have to force these attributes; they will just flow. This is the *agape* kind of love.

Income

There are millions of people using skills, but relatively few are using their GIFT. Someone using their GIFT will always rise above someone that is merely using a skill. We are told in Proverbs that "your GIFT will make room for you and bring you before great men." Why is that?

It is because greatness attracts greatness. Your GIFT is the master key to increasing your income.

In hard times employers will keep GIFTed employees and let the skilled ones go. Because a GIFT is a natural way of thinking, it requires less effort on the part of the GIFTed one, allowing for greater productivity. If you are paid for your time, your time will be more valuable than a non-gifted person's and your income will reflect it.

Since your GIFT is an expression of your thinking, you will not be constrained by merely "available" careers. Your unique way of thinking will be able to create new careers for your GIFT if necessary. As an example, many of the top careers available today didn't even exist twenty years ago. Someone with a GIFT created them.

Purpose

Employing your GIFT is your purpose. It really is that simple. So, if you are one who is looking for your purpose, just find your GIFT and your purpose will reveal itself.

Passion

You will not have to manufacture or put effort into sustaining passion when you know your GIFT. Everyone who knows their GIFT naturally desires to use it. As you begin to use your GIFT in a vision that you are emotional about, you will find that the passion to overcome any obstacle that gets in your way comes with the GIFT. What looks like a super-human effort to others is merely your passion expressing itself.

> Everyone who knows their GIFT naturally desires to use it.

Excellence

When you discover your GIFT you will naturally have a desire to use it. The joy you receive from giving your GIFT will make you want to give it as well and as often as possible. That is the genesis of excellence.

Employing your GIFT in excellence is what attracts others to you and what will produce income. Developing your GIFT as a good steward means devoting yourself to being the best at what God has given you. The world is full of people who are mediocre, or even good at what they do, but it is desperately short of people who work in excellence.

Relationship

People are naturally attracted to others who know who they are, know their GIFT, and know where they are going. This applies to friendships, business associates, and marriage.

> # There is nothing more attractive than a person with a plan, and who is engaged in their purpose.

There is nothing more attractive than a person with a plan, and who is engaged in their purpose. You don't have to wonder who they are and where they might take you, because no one's GIFT is complete by itself, but has to be used in combination with the GIFTs of others to fulfill a vision. That means that a person with a Special GIFT must have relationships with others. These kinds of relationships provide real peace. You never have to worry about the motive of someone employing their GIFT; it is evident.

There may be more benefits to knowing and employing your Special GIFT, but I think you'll agree that the FLIPPER benefits make it worthwhile to discover your GIFT.

The Greatest Benefit

Of the seven benefits of knowing your Special GIFT just explained in FLIPPER, love is the greatest. That might sound strange coming from a guy and a former Marine. For some reason, the concept of love seems to sound better when it comes from women with gentle spirits than from men. It also sounds reasonable when it comes from a pastor saying we should all love one another. I know those concepts of love were supposed to sound good, but to my ears, they were just talk that had no way of being implemented. It was nice stuff for someone else.

The kind of love that the Greeks called *agape* and is written about in the New Testament is really what we all strive for but have no idea how to find. It is an unconditional love that springs from your heart without having to force yourself to do, and with no thought of recompense. To my mind, people who could do that "agape thing" were saints because I sure didn't have it in me...or so I thought.

No matter how hard I tried to love people unconditionally, I either wanted something in return for my effort or I thought the people I was trying to love were losers. I know that sounds harsh, but to be completely honest with you being critical is part of my personality. My dilemma was that I wanted to serve a God whose only commandment was to love one another, but I had no idea how to do that.

Then I discovered my GIFT. Instead of trying to get something from people, I find I have a great desire to give my GIFT to them. As I employ my GIFT I find I have tolerance for others. I don't become offended at anything they say; instead, I do my best to communicate to them on their level. I do want the best for people when I am engaged in using my GIFT. When I'm busy with things outside of my GIFT, my regular critical self shows back up.

I was going to say if this works for me it will work for anyone, but it is more accurate to tell you that since it works for me it has worked for everyone I have been able to help find their GIFT. You were created to give this kind of love and you were given a GIFT that makes it possible. This kind of love is not some nebulous thing reserved for the do-gooders of the world. This kind of love is practical and possible for everyone.

Who wouldn't rather wake up to do what they were created for than face another day of struggle? Who wouldn't rather help people with their GIFT than constantly have to update skills in a task they barely put up with, just so they can make ends meet? Who wouldn't love the satisfaction that comes from success built on mutual benefit? Do what you were created to do, help people by giving your GIFT, and enjoy a fulfilled life. Then take notice of how much love flows out of you without having to think about it. Now that's a benefit!

Chapter 12
Your Choice

In deciding your direction in life, you probably sought the advice of your parents. I imagine at some point during the conversation they told you their greatest concern was for your happiness. If you have children of your own, you probably feel the same way—you want them to be happy. If you are married you probably want your spouse to be happy. I've heard it said, "If mama ain't happy, nobody's happy!" I think most husbands would agree.

But what makes you happy? What makes your spouse happy? Did you know you have more control over your happiness than you may have thought?

What Makes You Happy?

I realize this may seem harsh, but your happiness is the direct result of the choices you make. So, if you want to be happy you need to make good choices. If you want the happiness of others, then you want to enable them to make good choices. The challenge is that most of us don't spend much time thinking about what makes us happy. If you don't know what will make you happy, then making good choices becomes difficult.

> If you want to be happy you need to make good choices.

If you had to choose, which one of the following has the greatest influence on your happiness?

1. Security. There are many forms that security can take so I have given you three to choose from.

   - Physical Security—This is the kind of security that makes you feel safe in your home or the area in which you live. If you feel that your life is threatened, your chances of being happy are not very good. This is one of the reasons we have security alarms on our cars and some people buy security systems for their homes.

   - Emotional Security—If you are yelled at, berated, or live in an abusive situation, you are probably not going to feel very happy. A Father Fracture can also be the source of emotional insecurity if you didn't get the foundation of your identity that a good father figure can provide.

   - Financial Security—Many people don't feel secure if finances are stressed. It can feel like a threat to physical security if you can't pay your bills, and it is a fact that wellbeing rises along with income.

If you are safe, are not threatened emotionally, and money is not a concern, many would say they are happy.

2. Love. To love and to be loved are universal desires. If you do not know you are loved, or you don't have an object of your love, you won't be happy.

3. Purpose. Your purpose is to employ your Special GIFT. It is how you were designed to give and receive your unique kind of love. Living with purpose brings a degree of satisfaction to life that is missing otherwise.

4. Time to enjoy life. If your security needs are met, but you spend all your time working, then some free time to enjoy life may be

what would make you happy. For those who have found their purpose, this may not be as big of a deal, because the time they spend employing their GIFT is a labor of love and fun.

5. Achievement. For some people, having a sense of accomplishment and achievement is more important than for others. Even so, we all want to progress to some degree and this may be what you need to feel happy.

6. Creativity. The freedom and security to create are essential for some people to be happy. This could be hampered by bad relationships, a consuming or oppressive job, or just not knowing your GIFT.

7. Lack of stress. Let's face it, it is hard to be happy if you are under heavy stress. I know some people thrive on stress, but most of us don't. If you could just get rid of some stress you would be able to feel happy again.

8. Fun. For some, fun and happiness are the same things. If you aren't having fun you aren't happy.

9. Stuff. "He who has the most toys when he dies wins." This statement expresses what some people think will make them happy. Even though that is a very male-oriented statement, many women say the same thing, but in a different way. Stuff could be a new car or truck, a new hunting rifle, or it could be some new jewelry, shoes, or clothes.

10. Experiences. Even though people like to buy stuff to make them happy, many will say they would rather spend their money on experiences. A vacation, a date night, a night out with friends are some of the experiences that may make you feel happy.

11. Relationship. Happiness could also come from having someone with which to share your thoughts, dreams, hopes, ambitions.

Your happiness is the result of your choices, and your choices are the result of how you think. Therefore, your happiness is directly related to your Special GIFT. Your unique way of thinking is your Special GIFT. Not using it results in bad choices, ones that do not lead to happiness. For example, the first thing necessary for most people to be happy is to have their need for security satisfied.

> ## Your happiness is the result of your choices, and your choices are the result of how you think.

If your physical security is threatened because of where you live, then that is your choice. What can you do if you live in a high-crime area? You can choose to do nothing and put up with it, you can change the area through action, or you can move. Feeling insecure is your choice.

The same holds for emotional and financial security. If your emotional or financial situation is bad, you have much more control to change it than you may want to admit. If you are honest with yourself (not always easy), your past decisions played a part in the bad situation you are in now. What choices can you make today to allow yourself to be happier? You might be thinking, "I can't change; you don't know my situation." You are right, I don't know your situation, but changing your situation starts with changing yourself. In the words of Henry Ford, "If you think you can, or you think you can't, you are right." You have the choice to think you can change your situation.

Sometimes the people who tell you they want you to be happy don't mean it. A person who wants your happiness will help you to make good choices based on who you are and your GIFT. Unfortunately, people often say they want your happiness, but then proceed to guide you based on their desires. Sometimes they do it because they assume they know what makes you happy, and sometimes they want to manipulate you for their happiness. Whose advice you listen to is also your choice.

Choice and Your Special GIFT

Knowing your Special GIFT makes decision making easier. It makes deciding to be your real self easier than pretending to be someone you are not. It makes deciding to operate from your talents easier than choosing a career in which you constantly need to work on your weaknesses. Knowing your Special GIFT makes it easier to decide how you can make a real difference.

Knowing the special way that you think allows you to see how you may fit into an organization. It helps to make you feel your contributions to that organization have value. Your Special GIFT will also lead you to an organization with a mission, cause, or vision you can feel proud to be part of.

Without knowing your Special GIFT, you become subject to the same choices as the rest of the world. You may make choices based on the income potential of a job, the advice of a friend, or how close the job is to your home? Or you could make decisions based on the emotion of fear. You might be afraid that making the wrong choice will displease someone else, like your parents, your spouse, or a friend. You might choose to hide your real personality to "fit in." You might sacrifice your dreams on the altar of survival, accepting the fate of most whose only goal is to make it to the weekend.

That is exactly what I did after leaving the Marine Corps. Uncle Sam trained me and paid me to fly multimillion-dollar aircraft and blow up stuff. Even though I thought that was cool, there was no market for it in the civilian world. I had no idea how to translate my military skills to civilian-ease, nor did I have a clue what I wanted to do, so I relied on my recruiting firm to guide me. Bad choice!

Without discovering my personality, my strengths, or what I wanted, the recruiting firm I used chose to put me into a sales position with a pharmaceutical company. Why, you might ask? I think it was because they found a job opening for a pharmaceutical sales position and the recruiter convinced them I was a good fit. (Note: Recruiting firms make their money from the employers, not the potential employees.) It certainly wasn't because I possessed a GIFT for sales. The fear of not having a job and running out of income led me to choose to accept a job for which I wasn't well suited.

That bad decision on my part compounded when I quit the sales position in ten months with no backup plan...another bad decision. There was a bright side to the bad choices I made. Even though no one could advise me on how to make better choices, and I had not discovered the concept of having a GIFT yet, I was convinced there was a better way. My bad decisions set me on a quest to figure this out. I quickly learned that most of the people I talked to also made bad career decisions, but they had backup plans. Even though they weren't financially challenged, they were still living a life of quiet desperation. I was resolved not to live that way.

> # Knowing your Special GIFT puts you in a position of control when it comes to choosing a career.

Knowing your Special GIFT puts you in a position of control when it comes to choosing a career. It helps you by knowing what careers to look for, what visions to become a part of, and what careers to stay away from. If the economy is strong and there is little unemployment, your GIFT will be seen as a valuable asset to any company that needs what you can bring to the table. If the economy is down and there is much unemployment, then an employer who has a job opening is more likely to give it to someone who knows what they want and likes what they do than to employ someone who needs a job and will probably just do the minimum.

You have the choice to discover and employ your Special GIFT or to continue to do what everyone else does. It is easy to determine what most people do: just watch commercials on TV. Most people struggle through life, hopefully with a job they tolerate, to make it to the best part of their lives called retirement. The realities of retirement are wrapped in concerns about health care and not outliving your money. In other words, retirement is controlled fear.

That means that what everyone else does is to live in fear, only to retire in fear. To relieve the stress and emotion of fear most people distract themselves with some form of entertainment. It could be going to clubs or the tavern, golfing, fishing, traveling, vacationing in Disney World, or any number of a host of distractions to take their minds off of reality. Instead of living with purpose they drift through life, accepting their fate as if there is nothing they can do about it. It can lead to stress-related illnesses, depression, never feeling satisfied, and even thoughts of suicide.

All these are expressions of the ultimate fear of having no control over your destiny. Without purpose it can feel as if it is difficult to keep up in a world that keeps changing faster and faster. If you feel you have no control over your roller coaster life, you may want to get off the ride. However, that is just not true. You do have control over your destiny, and that control lies in the God-given GIFT you possess. You were blessed with a life and a means to succeed in that life.

What I Told You

You don't have to believe the myth that success in life only comes through struggle. At the beginning of the book, I called that myth the First System, a system in which there appeared to be only two ways to succeed. First: You can get a great education, work hard, and persevere for years. It involves a dream, a huge struggle, and the hope of a prize at the end. If you work hard enough and get the right breaks, you can escape from a level of just surviving to live life on your terms. The second way to succeed in this system is to be born into privilege. If you were born with an inheritance, then you can skip the struggle and go directly to the higher part of Maslow's Hierarchy of Needs.

The majority seem to buy into this myth, but there is a better way. Rather than struggling your way through life on the world's terms, you can choose to discover your Special GIFT and employ it. This means bucking the system that tells you to constantly update skills to remain relevant in an ever-changing world. Skills are learned and are developed to use knowledge effectively.

You can learn a skill in an area that you have limited or no natural ability. Using that skill requires a great deal of effort and concentration, and usually is not fun. A GIFT, on the other hand, is a natural ability that can be developed to greatness. It comes naturally to you with little or no effort because it is how you think. The time used in developing a GIFT is a joy. You do it so that you can be better at employing your GIFT. Skills are generally developed to allow you to survive and can be a mandatory part of your profession, whereas developing your Special GIFT is something you want to do so that you can become better at giving it.

> Your Special GIFT was not given to you by accident, but was chosen specifically for you to succeed in life. It is yours to use or yours to ignore.

Everyone has a Special GIFT. What others perceive as your GIFT is the manifestation of the very unique way that you think. The CliftonStrengths assessment developed by Gallup is a useful tool in determining your GIFT. The chances that someone else has the same strengths, and in the same order as yours is impossible. No one thinks like you.

Employing your Special GIFT, that unique way of thinking, is your purpose. Your Special GIFT was not given to you by accident, but was chosen specifically for you to succeed in life. It is yours to use or yours to ignore. If you choose to ignore it then you will be relegated to a life of struggle in the world's system. If you choose to use your GIFT you will discover your value and why people and organizations want what you have to offer.

You have the choice of how you want to employ your Special GIFT. As a visionary leader, you could start a new cause or business that requires the use of other people's GIFTs. If you don't have a vision of your own, you can employ your GIFT as part of someone else's vision. How you choose to operate in your Special GIFT determines the difference you will make.

Choosing to use your GIFT rather than going along with the world's system has many benefits. The acronym FLIPPER is a good way to remember that your Special GIFT is the key to **F**aithfulness, **L**ove, **I**ncome, **P**assion, **P**urpose, **E**xcellence, and **R**elationships in your life. Being somewhat process-oriented, I would say that the process would flow like this:

1. You have a Special GIFT. Being aware of this fact starts the discovery process:
    a. Discover your Special GIFT. You were born with it already in your possession.
    b. To do that you need to know who you *REALLY* are.

    c. You cannot know who you are if you have an unre-solved Father Fracture.

2. Your Purpose is to employ your Special GIFT. Finding out that you have a Special GIFT is awesome, but you need to use it.

    a. Saint Peter said, "As each one has received a special gift, employ it in serving one another as good stewards of the manifold grace of God."

    b. Mark Twain said, "The two most important days in your life are the day you are born, and the day you find out why."

3. The way that you will make a difference is by operating in your Special GIFT. Everyone wants to make a difference. The way you do that is by applying your purpose to a vision.

Caution: They Won't Understand

You can get into some of the best conversations talking to people about their Special GIFT. Once they find out they have one it is only natural for a person to want to know what theirs is. Of course, these conversations can get pretty deep and some people are not used to that. If the conversation takes place in the right setting, and they feel they won't be judged, I find that they usually open up and appreciate that someone actually takes the time to know them as they are.

I am constantly amazed at how willingly people will engage in discussions about deeply personal matters, especially since we live in an age where relationships are often conducted on social media and text messaging. Maybe we all want to connect at a deeper level and just need the right circumstances to do so. Discussing their Special GIFT appeals to people on a very meaningful level. It is an appeal to fill a void in themselves, one that could never be filled in a text message.

I would, however, caution you about asking someone about their Special GIFT without first explaining to them what that means. I have made the mistake of asking acquaintances if they knew their Special GIFT without first giving them some background information. Since the concept of a Special GIFT is foreign to most people, how could I expect them to answer the question? What I found was my acquaintances usually made up something they thought sounded good. One guy said he thought his GIFT was leadership because he thought he wanted to be a leader.

In actuality, he was not a leader at all; in fact, *leadership* is not one of the thirty-four talents that determine a person's GIFT as I describe it. Furthermore, he was a very good follower who loved people and was stressed to the point of illness because he was trying to be what he was not. My point is that people won't understand what you mean by telling them they have a Special GIFT without first preparing them for a subject they have probably never thought of before. They won't understand, and it could make them feel uncomfortable.

Talking with people about their Special GIFT is the most fun thing I am privileged to do. It always edifies them and makes them feel like the unique and special person they are. I find it helpful to mention there is an assessment they can take that will help them to understand their unique way of thinking. If they choose to take the assessment, then I really have something to talk with them about. That's when they begin to realize how much hope they have and just how wonderful life can be.

A person who begins to realize they have a Special GIFT might begin to realize they have been drifting through life. They might also realize they have been following someone else's plan for their life, one that will never bring them happiness. Knowing they can live with purpose and make a difference could be the greatest gift you could have ever given them. I can't begin to tell you how gratifying that can be for you.

Full Honors

As a Marine Captain, I once had the privilege to participate in a full honors funeral in Arlington National Cemetery. It was an overcast December morning as we began our march in front of the horse-drawn caisson containing the casket of a retired Marine Corps general. As light snow began to fall, all you could hear was the sound of fifty Marines marching in perfect unison. That sound echoed throughout the cemetery as if to let those that were buried there know they were soon to be joined by another fellow warrior.

As we approached the burial site I commanded the Marines to come to a halt. What followed next sent chills down my back. After a short eulogy from the Navy chaplain, the United States flag that draped the coffin was meticulously folded by the specially chosen pallbearers. The flag was folded in a perfect triangle with just the blue field and white stars showing and then handed to the wife on behalf of a grateful nation. This was followed by a twenty-one-gun salute and taps played by a lone bugler. The final tribute to the general was a cannonade. Howitzer cannons were fired in succession as an ultimate display of honor to one who had served his country. It was a most solemn and moving tribute.

After we marched off, and the grieving widow and family had left the cemetery, the final part of the process took place. The grave was completed; the grass was carefully laid and a plain white marble headstone was placed to mark the grave. The only thing that differentiated the general's marker from the perfectly aligned headstones that surrounded it was his name and two dates. The date of his birth and the date of his death were separated by a small space. That small space represented his life. I never knew the general, but if his funeral was any indicator of his life, it was an awesome one.

Everyone has a birth date and everyone will have that second date on their tombstone, but it is the space that separates them that counts most. What you do with yours is largely a matter of your choice. You can choose to drift with the flow of life, accepting whatever comes along, or you can choose to use your Special GIFT and make a difference.

What's Next?

Now that you have an idea of what a Special GIFT is and its potential benefits, you might ask yourself, "So, what's next?" It is great to know that you were blessed with a Special God-given GIFT that was designed just for you to help you realize your heart's desire. It is even better if you decide to do something with the information you have just read. Deciding to do something great with your life is awesome, but there is something even better. To illustrate my point, let me tell you the story of the three cats.

When Mary and I were newlyweds we lived in a nice neighborhood in Encinitas, California. The development we lived in was brand new and all of the neighbors moved in at about the same time as we did. The new homes did not come with landscaping so on weekends you would find most of the neighbors doing the same thing as us...working on our yards. That meant putting up six-foot-tall wood privacy fences. I thought the fences were so that the neighbors couldn't see into our tiny backyard, but I found out there was another reason.

It seemed that almost everyone on our street had pets. We had a golden retriever and a black lab, the guys across the street had two boxers, and everyone else had cats. We would often walk our dogs with the neighbors' dogs in the canyon behind our house, frequently running into the native Southern California wildlife. It was not unusual to see tarantulas, a rattlesnake or two, and coyotes on our walks.

The cats in the neighborhood were unbelievably lazy. It was not unusual to have to drive my car around one of the neighborhood felines that was stretched out taking a nap in the middle of the road. Then one day things started to change for our local cats. The coyotes discovered them. Only a few tufts of cat hair remained where the lazy street cat once slept. The guys across the street, and next to the couple with the boxers, had their front window screen pushed in by a coyote that grabbed their cat off the windowsill.

That is when I discovered the second purpose of the privacy fences. The remaining cats in our neighborhood realized their lives were in danger, especially after dark. As a defensive maneuver they would hang out on the top of the six-foot fences. Sometimes there would be a few of them on the same fence and they could get pretty noisy.

One night our backyard sounded like the cats were getting way too rowdy. I went outside to find three cats perched on the top of my fence. Not being a cat lover, I picked up an old boot and threw it at the cats to scare them off. The boot hit the fence and two of the cats decided to get off.

How many cats were left on my fence? If you say one you would answer the way most would, but the answer is three. Just because two of the cats decided to get off the fence does not mean they actually did.

You probably figured out I made up that story. The part about the coyotes was true, but not the three cats. That was to get you to realize that just making a decision isn't enough. You need to follow through with what you have decided. Deciding to pursue your Special GIFT is a great decision, and I don't want to leave you hanging there.

There are seven steps to making a difference by finding your purpose and you will find them in my book, *The Joe Purpose Master Key*. To get the most from *The Joe Purpose Master Key* I strongly suggest you take the DISC personality assessment and the CliftonStrengths assessment from Gallup. The assessments will help you discover your Special GIFT and the seven steps will show you what to do with it.

Resources

As a Man Thinketh, James Allen

Before you Quit Your Job, Robert Kiyosaki

Cash Flow Quadrant, Robert Kiyosaki

Deadly Emotions, Dr. Don Colbert

Fatherless America, David Blankenhorn

In Pursuit of Purpose, Myles Monroe

Master Key to Riches, Napoleon Hill

Rich Dad Poor Dad, Robert Kiyosaki

StrengthsFinder 2.0, Tom Rath

Strengths Based Leadership, Tom Rath

The 5 Love Languages, Gary Chapman

The GIFT in You, Caroline Leaf

The Holy Bible, God

The New Retirementality, Mitch Anthony

Think and Grow Rich, Napoleon Hill

What Americans Really Want...Really, Frank Luntz

Who Do You Think You Are Anyway, Robert Rohm

About the Author

Thomas J. Gilroy is an author, lecturer, and businessman. He and his wife Mary reside in Foxfire Village, NC. He grew up in Dale City, VA and attended the University of Virginia before being commissioned as a Marine Officer. His military specialty was as an attack helicopter pilot, where he received the nickname "TJ."

TJ entered the business world after his Marine Corps career, eventually becoming an executive in the tactical equipment industry. He and Mary now own JoePurpose.com and TJGilroy.com, working with people to help them discover their purpose and mentoring those that are seeking.

Early in his business career TJ found that asking better questions resulted in receiving better answers. Whether asking questions of his parents, his Commanding Officers in the Marine Corps, his wife Mary, his mentor Jack, his business associates, or friends, or most importantly, the Holy Spirit, the same always held true; ask good questions, get good answers. He also found that the times of his life where he was just drifting, or was frustrated, were also the times when he stopped asking questions.

Subsequently, the answers he found and put into practice are now available to you. His ardent hope for you is that you find your purpose and that you make the difference God intended.